A Handbook of Bible Customs for Kids

Lamps, Scrolls & Goatskin Bottles

Handbook of
Customs for Kids

Lamps, Scrolls & Goatskin Bottles

Over **70** fun-and-easy
activities and crafts
for Bible lessons

by Julia B. Hans

STANDARD
PUBLISHING
Cincinnati, Ohio

Dedication

To Michael, Kristin, and Abigail

Lamps, Scrolls, and Goatskin Bottles: A Handbook of Bible Customs for Kids
Published by Standard Publishing, Cincinnati, Ohio
A division of Standex International Corporation
© 2000 Julia B. Hans
All rights reserved.
Printed in the United States of America
07 06 05 04 03 02 01 00   5 4 3 2
All Scripture quotations are taken from the King James Version.

CREDITS
Acquisition Editor: Ruth Frederick
Cover design and illustrations by Liz Howe
Interior illustrations by Jan Knudson
Interior design by Jeff Richardson
All photos except for the cover photo "Bethlehem, From Shepherd's Fields"
(Robert Harding Picture Library, London, ©1986 Biblical Archaeology Society)
were taken by Mark Ziese (©2000 Mark Ziese).

Acknowledgments

The author gratefully acknowledges those who have helped see this book into print. I wish to thank Larry LoVerme for his research assistance, Laura LoVerme for enthusiastically proofreading the text, Jon Bennett for his help with chapter 5, Edwidge Fairweather and Patricia LoVerme for helping to develop games and crafts, Raj Hans for faithfully praying for this project, to my mother Claudia Dunbar for encouraging me as a writer, and to family and friends who have heartened me with kind words along the way—thank you. Thanks to Ruth Frederick at Standard Publishing for accepting this project, and to Bruce Stoker for his fine editorship. I am especially indebted to my husband, Ravi Hans, not only for his unflinching support over the years, but also for the many ways he contributed to this project—from critical proofreading, to developing games, to showing me how to tie a turban. Thanks, *hanje,* for being an example to me and to our children of Christian love, believing, and service. Finally, I am most grateful to Almighty God for his boundless love, grace, and mercy, and to my Lord and Savior, Jesus Christ, the mediator between God and man.

Table of Contents

Introduction

The Bible is book written in an Eastern culture, and it is filled with customs and idioms unfamiliar to most Western readers. It speaks of elders who sit in the gates, mourners who sit in sackcloth and ashes, and men who gird their loins before running. In the ancient Near East, shaving off a man's beard was an insult, and "heaping coals of fire on his head" was considered a blessing. People walked on the rooftops and bathed outdoors. What does it all mean? The answers to these riddles and more lie in the pages of *Lamps, Scrolls, and Goatskin Bottles.*

Learning about ancient Near Eastern customs is not only intriguing, it is essential for any serious Bible student, for ignorance in this field often leads to error or to confusion. For instance, one children's

book shows Rahab's house with two spies neatly tucked under sheaves of grain—all suspended from an A-shaped roof! If only the artist had known that in biblical times, roofs were flat! Tradition might say that the baby Jesus was wrapped in rags because his parents were poor, but the truth is that he was wrapped in swaddling clothes to represent both his regal status and his devotion to God (see chapter 5). And while some have said that Jesus Christ and his disciples stole grain, the custom of the time permitted people to eat grain whenever they passed by a field (see chapter 6). Understanding ancient Near Eastern customs, then, becomes tantamount to "rightly dividing the Word of truth."

For teachers, the topic is a natural in the classroom, whether at home, at school, or at church, because kids are fascinated by different cultures. Children want to know what type of tunic Mary wore, how Sarah baked unleavened bread, and what Joseph made in his carpenter shop. Using the activities in *Lamps, Scrolls, and Goatskin Bottles,* you can help students see for themselves how ancient Near Eastern people lived. Make a tent dweller's tent, a goatskin bottle, and a clay lamp. Or cook lentil stew, write on a leather scroll with a reed pen, make a phylactery, or design your own signet ring. Act out certain manners and customs, like the Middle Eastern way of "knocking" at the door or separating wheat from chaff by using a winnowing fork.

There are several ways to use this book. Read the chapters to gain an overview of Near Eastern life—what people ate, the types of clothes they wore, or how they raised their children. Or hone in on a specific topic or custom by studying the corresponding Scripture references in each chapter. Those who homeschool their children can develop their own unit studies from this book, and teachers can augment their Bible curriculum. Look up the Scripture references within each chapter to see how a particular custom applies. Finally, use this book as a springboard for further study. Just as the Bible is inexhaustible, so is this subject!

Finally, a word about the contents of this book. Because this is a small book about a big topic, certain subjects had to be omitted or whittled down. Chapters on politics, currency, and transportation, for instance, are notably absent. In deciding what to include in this book, I considered two things: relevancy to the Scriptures and appeal to children. Writing about shepherds and farming seemed reasonable because the Bible abounds with references to shepherding and to agriculture. And although the Bible doesn't talk much about toys and games, I figured kids would find that topic interesting. (What child wouldn't want to know that kids in Ur of the Chaldees played hopscotch and leapfrog or that Roman boys played with tiny tin soldiers?)

In the end, I hope that *Lamps, Scrolls, and Goatskin Bottles* helps you appreciate ancient Near Eastern customs in the Bible and, in so doing, better understand—and believe—the Book of Life.

"So then faith cometh by hearing, and hearing by the word of God" (Romans 10:17).

Julia B. Hans

Chapter One

Dwelling Places

"For we know that, if our earthly house of this tabernacle were dissolved, we have a building of God, a house not made with hands, eternal in the heavens" (2 Corinthians 5:1).

"Put your back into it, Shamir," Remphah calls to his son. "That pole must stand straight like the mighty oak, or we'll be sleeping in puddles tonight."

A boy of ten summers pushes with all his might against the nine-foot pole, his tanned face turning red under the strain. His father looks at the thick, black clouds overhead, then quickly straightens the remaining tent poles.

"I've almost got it now, Father," Shamir calls between grunts. He thrusts his shoulder into the limb and pushes. Salty drops of sweat sting his eyes. His leg muscles quiver beneath the weight of the heavy pole, but Shamir stands his ground. With one final shove, he pushes the pole erect.

"Good work, son," Remphah says. "But there's no time to lose. Help me get her staked before the rains come."

Remphah squats near a wooden stake driven deep into the ground and holds out his hand expectantly to the boy. Shamir grabs the leather loop hanging from the hem of the tent and stretches it out to his father. Remphah slips the loop over the stake, as thunder rumbles in the distance.

"Hurry!" Remphah shouts, running to the next loop. "Let's get the others tied. Those clouds look like they're about to burst like old wineskins."

Shamir and his father tie the second loop, and then another and another until all sixteen bands are safely anchored. At last the tent stands taut, its black goatskin walls rippling in the wind.

Fat raindrops plop to the ground as Shamir ducks under a tent flap after his father. Remphah lights a small clay lamp, then the two stretch out on camel hair cushions. "Let the rains come," Remphah says, smiling at his son. "Tonight, we will be safe and warm in our house of hair."

Tents: Houses of Hair

Like Shamir and his father, many people in the ancient Near East were nomads, tent dwellers who moved from place to place in search of water and food. Living in tents is as old as the Bible itself, going back before the days of Noah. The patriarchs Abraham, Isaac, and Jacob lived in tents, and so did others in the Bible, such as Noah, Moses, and his father in law, Jethro. In wartime, armies camped in tent cities. Shepherds built for themselves temporary shelters whenever pasturing their flocks far from home (see Jeremiah 6:3). But unlike the sturdy tent of the nomad, a shepherd's tent was flimsy, quick to erect and to dismantle. These tents came apart so quickly that Middle Eastern people say something done quickly is "like a shepherd's tent"—like we might say, "quick as a wink."

Tent dwellers made their tents out of goatskin and tree limbs. They staked the tent by driving long wooden planks through leather loops sewn along the tent borders. Or ropes were tied to the corners of the tent and anchored with large boulders. To make the hides waterproof, the tent dweller soaked the hides in water and then let them dry in the sun, thereby shrinking them. Prepared hides are sometimes called "curtains" (see Isaiah 54:2).

Although goatskin tents sheltered people from the elements, they didn't protect them from their enemies. Therefore, tent dwellers often camped together in tribes or clans, pitching their tents in a circle with their livestock protected in the middle. A sheik, or clan ruler, would plant his distinguishing spear outside his tent. While a sheik might have a large tent, historians say the average tent in Bible times was roughly the size of a two-car garage. Women rarely had their own tents; only the wife of a rich or powerful man might have her own dwelling. Jacob's two wives, Rachel and Leah, and their two servants each had their own tents—an indication of Jacob's considerable wealth (Genesis 31:33).

Tents were ordinarily divided into two sections: the front half for men and guests, and the back half for women and children. According to ancient Near Eastern custom, men were forbidden to enter into the woman's side of the tent. During hot afternoon hours, tent dwellers often sat in the "door of the tent," meaning a tent flap. There they could enjoy the shade within and the breeze without. Note how Abraham was resting in "the tent door in the heat of the day" when the three angels appeared to him (Genesis 18:1).

Inside a tent dweller's tent you'd likely find a few rugs or mats, some camel hair cushions, and a few kitchen items, such as a stone flour mill, cruse of oil, clay pitchers and bowls, and a leather bucket for drawing water. The tent dweller's ubiquitous oil lamp would also be on hand. Filled with olive oil, these lamps were often small enough to carry in the palm of the hand. These looked like small, shallow clay bowls that often have their edges pinched together at as many as three or four places to hold a wick of braided flax (a plant fiber used for making linen).

In the ancient Near East, people believed that sleeping without a lighted lamp was a sign of poverty. Middle Easterners also believe that light represents the presence of God; they consider it a disgrace to let the lamplight go out. Therefore, ancient Near Eastern women or girls would make sure that a light burned continually in their homes. Young girls might tie a string from one pinched "finger" of the lamp to a tiny cruse of oil. The lighted wick would be able to burn for hours, giving off a pleasant aroma.

In addition to his lamp, a tent dweller would have several goatskin bottles on hand to carry or store water, milk, or wine. To make a goatskin bottle, the animal hide was cleaned, stretched over a rack, scraped smooth, and then soaked in water. It was made waterproof by drying it in the sun. Four of the five openings (at the animal's legs and neck) were tightly tied with ropes, and the fifth spout was capped off with a wooden or leather stopper. Tent dwellers still use this type of bottle today.

In biblical times, the life of a tent dweller was ever changing, as he moved from place to place, carrying his home and belongings with him. In parts of Arabia today, Bedouin families still live in goatskin tents just as Abraham, Isaac, and Jacob did. (Bedouins are tent dwellers of a specific people group found in Saudia Arabia, Syria, and Northern Africa.) They say they love the freedom of having the earth for a floor and the sky for a ceiling. To them, their "house of hair" is home.

Search the Scriptures

In Isaiah 38:12, we read that Hezekiah's age is "removed from me as a shepherd's tent," meaning that Hezekiah lost his health quickly or suddenly.

Psalm 119:83 says, "For I am become like a bottle in the smoke; yet do I not forget thy statutes." In Middle Eastern homes, goatskin bottles might be hung from the ceiling when not in use. And because cooking was sometimes done indoors, smoke from the fire would rise to the ceiling, making the skin appear like a goat suspended in smoke. The picture was one of destitution and helplessness. The Psalmist is saying that although he may appear helpless or distraught, he will not forget God's Word.

Bedouins setting up a tent in Jordan

Houses of Mud

Over time, the children of Israel exchanged their tents for more permanent dwellings made out of mud, stone, and timber. Archaeologists believe that many people in Bible times lived in single-room, mud-brick houses with a fenced yard or courtyard. The flat roofs on these houses were made from mud, straw, and timber, and the narrow windows were placed high up on the wall to discourage intruders. Although well suited to the Middle Eastern climate, brick houses such as these were not problem-free. In heavy rains, the mortar might turn soapy, and the bricks could slip apart. In dry weather, bricks crumbled. Thieves could literally "break through" by taking apart a wall (Matthew 6:19), and snakes could easily slither through crevices and holes (see Amos 5:19). Repairs on these mud homes were constant.

Furnishings within a brick house might include stools, rugs, and a few mats. According to ancient custom, interior walls were usually painted white with a chalky lime mixture but were kept bare. In some parts of the ancient Near East, people would not decorate their walls or hang drawings because they feared they might be tempted to worship an image instead of worshiping God. Likewise, they did not adorn their home's exterior for fear of attracting robbers.

Nearly every village home would have a courtyard. This exterior room served as barnyard, kitchen, or storage pantry. In harsh weather, the family's animals were sheltered there. (Although frail animals were sometimes allowed inside the home for protection, people in Bible times did not ordinarily keep house pets. Dogs were despised animals, kept outside city limits. Cats were disliked because of their

Mud-brick walls in Ottoman village in Jawa

association with idol worship.) Meals were often cooked in the courtyard, and dried grains and other foodstuff might be stored there as well. In cold weather, families warmed themselves around the fireplace, a shallow pit filled with hot coals, normally located in a draft-free corner of the courtyard.

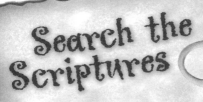

Search the Scriptures

Cisterns, or underground water collectors, were lined with stone or lime to make them watertight. In a broken or cracked cistern, water would leak out and seep into the ground. The prophet Jeremiah compared God to a fountain—an endless supply of water—yet compared man-made idols to a broken cistern that can hold no water (Jeremiah 2:13).

Plaster covered mud-brick walls

Rooftops

In the ancient Near East, roofs were used nearly as much as the living quarters below. In pleasant weather, families slept there with only the starry sky for a ceiling. Sometimes a permanent or temporary shelter was built on the rooftop to give people additional shade during the intense summer heat. These upper rooms (sometimes called "booths"—see Nehemiah 8:16) would typically be offered to a house guest as a gesture of hospitality and respect. Ancient Near Eastern people also prayed up on their roofs at set hours of the day: "On the morrow, as they went on their journey, and drew nigh unto the city, Peter went up upon the housetop to pray about the sixth hour" (Acts 10:9).

With many village houses joined together, the rooftop surface was often large enough for people to take their evening strolls. In ancient times, people also walked on top of city walls, and kings could enjoy a promenade on their sprawling palace rooftops. From that high vantage point, one could see nearly everything below—either someone approaching (2 Samuel 18:24-27) or a woman bathing (2 Samuel 11:2).

During harvest season, fruits and grains would sometimes be laid out on the roof to dry. That's where Rahab hid the two spies under the flax, a plant fiber used for making linen that was drying on her roof (Joshua 2:6). And with stairs or a ladder reaching to the street below, roofs provided quick getaways. Middle Eastern people say that you can jump from roof to roof and escape down a ladder while your enemy is still searching the house below. This is sometimes called "the road of the roofs."

To protect people from tumbling off these flat roofs, parapets or low walls were constructed around the roof's perimeter. The Law of Moses commanded that people build these protective barriers (called a "battlement" in Deuteronomy 22:8). Heavy rains also posed a threat to safety. During monsoon season, torrential rains could wreak havoc on flat roofs, causing some to collapse. After a heavy rain, a man would spread another layer of mud on his rooftop, smoothing it out with a large stone roller. Visitors to the Bible lands say that you can see these rollers in the corner of nearly every rooftop. So while leaky roofs were always a nui-

Notice how the mud roof is supported by layers of sticks over heavy timbers.

sance in the ancient Near East, they were hardly ever a surprise.

Sometimes grass seed got accidentally mixed in with the mud, and a carpet of unwanted grass grew on top (see 2 Kings 19:26 and Psalm 129:6). Middle Eastern people consider it a curse to have grass growing on their roofs—they say they'd pluck up every blade by hand, if necessary. If their lofty lawn got out of hand, they might let animals go up and graze there.

A network of these one-room, brick houses made up the villages of the ancient Near East. With their flat, mud roofs and crumbling brick walls, country houses required constant attention. Yet throughout the Bible lands, these simple homes provided people with adequate shelter. Many historians believe that Jesus Christ lived in a house like this while growing up in Nazareth.

Search the Scriptures

When Jesus Christ instructed his disciples "that which ye have spoken in the ear in closets shall be proclaimed upon the housetops" (Luke 12:3), he meant that the message would be heralded for all to hear. Important news was announced on rooftops in Bible times.

Leaky roofs were commonplace in the Middle East, so when the proverb compares the nuisance of a dripping roof to an argumentative woman, every one could relate! (Proverbs 27:15)

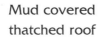

Mud covered thatched roof

City Dwellings

Historians say that after the first century A.D., many people lived in cities like Antioch. The third largest city of the ancient world, Antioch had its own lighting system, racetrack, fifty-foot skyscrapers, and several roads paved in marble! What would a house in Antioch look like? According to archaeologists, a typical city house in New Testament times was made from mud bricks like the hut in the village, but a city dwelling was usually more elaborate. Some stood two or three stories high. Others had numerous rooms built around lush courtyards. Porches, guest chambers, and windows with fancy latticework were commonplace.

The courtyard was the heart of the city home. People used these garden rooms for nearly everything: bathing, cooking, eating, and entertaining. Most houses were designed with the courtyard in the center with rooms arranged around it. Cisterns, or wide holes lined with stone, were used to collect water. These were important features of nearly every courtyard, for a common water supply was scarce in the city. Some of the more lavish courtyards were filled with fruit trees like pomegranate or apricot, as well as flowering vines, bushes, and even water fountains.

Note the narrow streets of ancient cities like this one in Beer-sheba.

Search the Scriptures

Because dogs were despised animals in the lands and times of the Bible, to be called a "dog" was a terrible insult. When a man cursed King David (2 Samuel 16:9), David's servant Abishai called the man a "dead dog"—one of the lowest insults you could sling at a man! When the crippled Mephibosheth came before King David, he called himself a "dead dog"—evidence of his humility before the king (2 Samuel 9:8).

Uncovering an ancient stone roof roller

Gates

"Gates" in the Bible can mean several things, such as a door, an archway, or an entrance to a city. To reach a home's inner courtyard, for instance, you'd likely have to go through a series of portals or gates. Middle Easterners built this type of gate low, for they say, "a high gate is an open invitation to robbers."

Gates could also be an opening to a city. These gateways buzzed with activity. People congregated there to hear news, and a prophet might declare his message in the city gates, like Jeremiah did in the gates of Jerusalem (see Jeremiah 17:19). City elders often settled disputes there. When Boaz wanted to settle a matter concerning Elimelech's field, he took ten elders and sat in the gate of the city, for he knew disputes were settled there (see Ruth 4:1, 2). The Law of Moses also made provisions for such matters: "Judges and officers shalt thou make thee in all thy gates, which the Lord thy God giveth thee, throughout thy tribes: and they shall judge the people with just judgment" (Deuteronomy 16:18).

In ancient times, a gate could also be a door to a city. On a walled city, gates were massive, usually made from wood, metal, or stone. City gates were typically secured with locks and bars with a keeper or watchman standing vigil at all times. If two walls encircled a city, there would be two gates with a space between—a favorite hiding spot in ancient times, and possibly the place where David hid when he was running from Absalom (see 2 Samuel 18:24). Because large walled cities would have several gates, prominent ones were often named.

There are several ancient customs involving gates or doors, some still practiced in the Middle East today. For instance, house doors were usually opened before sunrise and closed at sunset as a gesture of hospitality. Door keys, ordinarily about the size of a ruler, were often tied to strings and carried over the shoulder. The ancient Near Eastern idiom "to lay a key upon the shoulder," meant to transfer authority to someone. When Eliakim was about to inherit the kingdom, Isaiah said, "And the key of the house of David will I lay upon his shoulder" (Isaiah 22:22).

Historians and experts in Near Eastern customs say that in the Near East, knocking at the door involved more than just rapping on wood with your knuckles. When a Near Eastern person went to visit someone, he would stand at the door and call out to those inside, waiting until someone recognized his voice. A servant or porter would stand at the door listening to the visitor's voice. If the porter recognized the voice, he would open the door. You can see references to or examples of this custom in Luke 13:25, 26, in Revelation 3:20, and in Acts 12:13-15. In the passage in Acts, the servant girl Rhoda, even though she recognized Peter's voice, did not remember to open the door because she was so amazed by Peter's deliverance from prison.

Compared to the sparse country house, the city home had many trappings. Besides numerous kitchen items including metal utensils, houses were often furnished with divans (raised seats), tables and chairs, stools, benches, canopy beds, or even tubs for bathing. Bronze or copper lamps on tall stands replaced the tent dweller's tiny clay lamp. Historians tell us that wealthy city dwellers had plush carpets, inlaid wood, or hand-hewn stone on their floors, and they decorated their walls and ceilings with fancy tapestries.

In New Testament times, cities like Antioch teemed with life. Thousands of people crowded the narrow streets as merchants hawked their wares in the marketplace. Heavy-laden donkeys brayed under their master's rod, and barefooted children ran up and down the road of the roofs. Because Antioch was along a major trade route, travelers from Ephesus or Jerusalem would often stop there for provisions. Everywhere they went, people talked about the followers of Jesus of Nazareth, whom many were now calling "Christians" (Acts 11:26).

Search the Scriptures

In Acts 12:13-16, Rhoda identified Peter by his voice. She didn't recognize Peter by looking at him through a peephole. She recognized his voice and then ran to tell the others.

Princes and judges often sat in the city gates where court was frequently held and disputes settled. When Lot sat in the gates of Sodom, that meant he was an involved citizen, perhaps even a city elder (see Genesis 19:1). Because judgment often took place in the city gates, the phrase "sat in the gate" came to mean having authority or power in that city. The phrase "gates of hell" in Matthew 16:18 could possibly refer to the "power of hell" and not a literal door.

Even the streets of modern Middle Eastern cities, such as this one in the Muslim quarter of Jersusalem (right), are quite narrow.

Goatskin Tent

Materials Needed:

- ½ yard black material, such as broadcloth, cotton, or felt (available in fabric stores)
- two 3-foot-long, ¼-inch dowels (available in craft or hardware stores)
- rectangular Styrofoam board about 10 inches by 12 inches (available in department or craft stores)
- scissors
- ruler and chalk for measuring
- string, twine, or yarn
- hole punch
- 4 rocks about the size of golf balls

Note: This tent can also be made outdoors. Substitute twigs for the dowels and stick them into the ground. Use burlap and twine for a realistic look.

Directions:

1. Cut the dowels into six 6-inch lengths and three 9-inch lengths.
2. Place dowels into Styrofoam board as shown.
3. Cut fabric as follows:
   (A) one piece 15 inches by 15 inches
   (B) two pieces 15 inches long by 4 inches wide
   (C) two pieces 7 inches long by 9 inches wide
4. Punch holes in fabric as shown, no less than ½ inch from edge to avoid tearing.
5. Tie (B) to (A) on both sides as shown.
6. Tie (C) to remaining sides of (A) as shown.
7. Tie a length of string from each corner of (A) to a rock.
8. Make a 3-inch cut in the middle of one side of (C). Pin back one side to make a door flap.

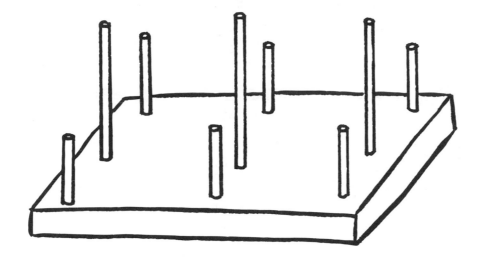

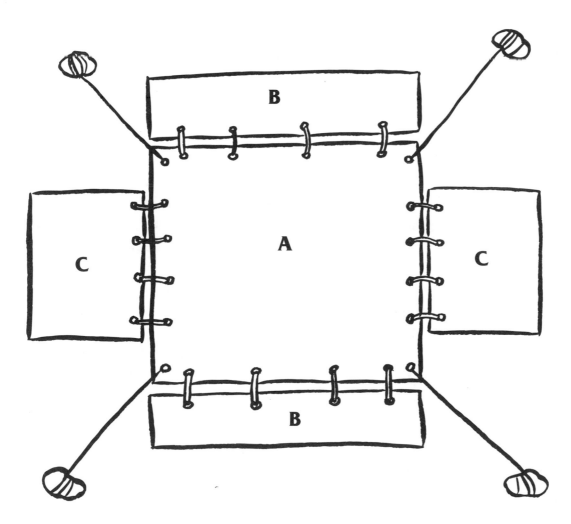

Making a Mud Brick House

Materials Needed:

- One package of terra-cotta modeling clay
- knife
- four to ten twigs for roof
- toothpicks
- piece of green felt or dried grass/hay
- water (for softening clay)

Directions:

Lay out newspaper before you get started. This clay is messy and can stain.

You can make your house out of individual bricks (keep in mind that this will take a long time to complete), or you can construct it using long strips with the edges scored to look like bricks. To do this:

1. Flatten the clay to your desired thickness (approximately ¼ inch) and cut ½-inch-wide strips to your desired length.

2. Stack these strips until you reach the desired height of the house. You might want to overlap pieces at the corner and push a toothpick through all the layers in each corner for extra support.

3. To make the roof, lay the twigs across roof making sure the tips jut out from the edge.

4. Lay the felt roof across the twigs.

5. To make the parapet, place four strips of clay on edge on top of the felt. (You might want to cut half-circle holes in the bottom of the parapet before you place it.)

6. To make a staircase, cut another strip of clay and cut steps into it. Wet one side of the steps slightly and stick it to a side wall. (You can fasten the steps to the wall with toothpicks.)

7. Cut out a door and windows. (You can also add courtyard walls using strips of clay bricks similar to the way you made the walls of the house.)

8. Before the clay dries too much, score the edges of the clay strips to make a brick pattern.

9. Let the house dry in the sun for several days.

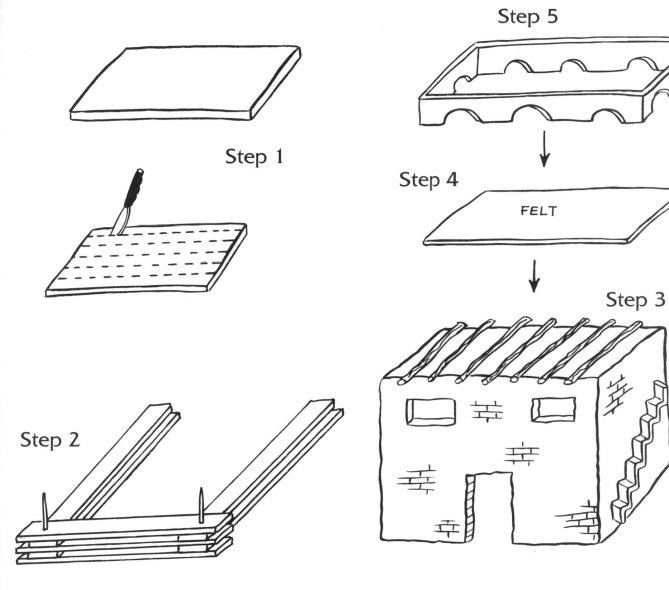

Step 1

Step 2

Step 5

Step 4

FELT

Step 3

Paper Bag House

Materials Needed:

- large paper grocery bag (with no writing on it if possible)
- scissors
- hot glue gun
- empty spool of thread
- ruler and pencil
- 2 pieces of felt—one piece brown or green, one blue
- about 15 to 20 jumbo craft sticks

Directions:

1. Cut off the bottom portion of the bag to make a rectangular house about 8 inches high.
2. Glue craft sticks inside the bag to make the structure sturdier, two per corner and one on each fold in the bag if necessary.
3. Cut the windows and a door as shown.
4. Measure and cut the felt to cover the roof, then glue it onto the roof. (You can use brown felt if you want a mud roof or green if you'd prefer a grassy roof.)
5. Cut two pieces for the parapet. The total length should equal the sum of both the short and long wall lengths, or the perimeter of the whole house.
6. Cut out half circles in the base of the parapets as shown.
7. Glue the parapets along edges of roof.
8. For the courtyard, cut a piece from the remaining pieces of the bag that is 6 inches by the length of the long wall of the house. Place this in front of house. (It is not attached to house.)

9. Cut three pieces for mud walls of courtyard: two pieces at 4 inches by the length of a short wall and one piece at 4 inches by the length of the long wall.
10. Fold down about ⅛ to ¼ inch of each edge of the mud walls and attach the walls to the courtyard floor with glue. Glue sticks inside for extra support. Keep in mind that the walls will be rounded.
11. To make the roof roller, you will need an empty spool of thread and a chenille wire. Insert the wire through the spool, tie the ends at the top. Snip off any excess. The spool should roll smoothly. Place the roller at a corner of the rooftop.

13. To make a bed you will need a 6 inch by 4 inch piece of blue felt and two craft sticks. Glue a craft stick to each end. Roll up the bed and place it in an inside corner of the house.

To add details, draw a set of stairs on the side of the house, or make a staircase out of blocks and place it alongside a wall. You can also draw lines on the courtyard walls to make them look more like bricks. Make other houses of different sizes and join them together—see if their roofs match up. Place plastic farm animals in the courtyard for a realistic look.

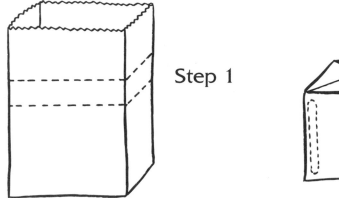 Step 1

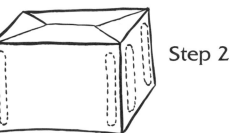 Step 2

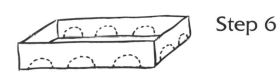 Step 6

 Step 8 & 9

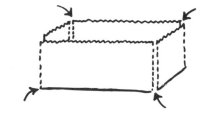 Step 10

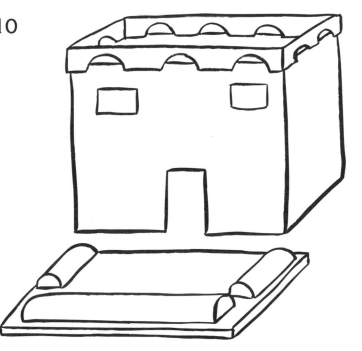

Family Spear

Materials Needed:

- Large tree branch that is about as tall as you are (something like a walking stick)
- Knife for whittling (children who are carving should always be under adult supervision)
- 8 inch by 11 inch piece of cardboard
- Markers or crayons
- Glue
- Tape
- Small nail or thumb tack
- Other decorations such as glitter, bobbles, beads, etc.

Directions:

1. Once you've found a tree limb about your size, cut away any extra twigs or leaves so that you have a smooth spear.
2. Whittle one end to a point so that it can be thrust into the ground.
3. Cut the cardboard into any shape you choose, such as a diamond, then decorate it with your family crest and other decorations (glitter, beads, string, etc.). (If you don't have a family crest, make one up. Find out interesting facts about your ancestors. Were they fishermen, bankers, or preachers? Then draw pictures on your crest that represent your family. For instance, let's say your ancestors were Portuguese fishermen who later came to the United States and became merchants. You could draw a picture of fish or boats with the flag of Portugal behind it, then a picture of a store with the stars and an eagle over it.)
4. Finally, attach your crest to the spear with strong tape or hot glue. Or you might attach it with a very small nail or thumb tack.

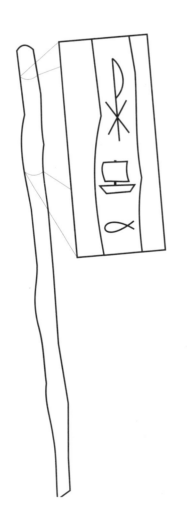

Clay Lamp

Materials Needed:

- Hard-drying modeling clay. (DAS terra-cotta is ideal and is found in better toy stores.)
- Modeling knife (a butter knife will do)
- Toothpick
- 4-inch piece of twine
- Newspapers and protective clothing

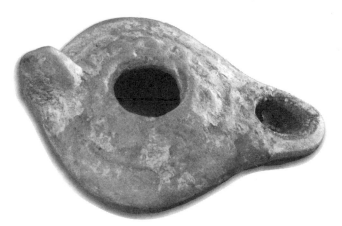

Directions:

1. Spread out newspapers and cover yourself with a paint smock:
2. Take a tennis-ball-size piece of clay (about 3 to 4 ounces) and roll into a ball.
3. Flatten out the ball and form a shallow bowl. From the bowl, shape the lamp by pinching together at least one small section to hold a wick.
4. Decorate with knife and toothpick in whatever pattern you wish.
5. Let dry according to directions (often 24 hours or more).
6. Once the lamp is dry, paint it or leave it a natural color.
7. Place the twine wick in the pinched end. (Remember, do not light this lamp. It is for instructional purposes only.)

"Where Do I Go?"

Color in each of the items. Then cut them out and attach them to either the Bible Lands Village or the Modern village.

Dwelling Places

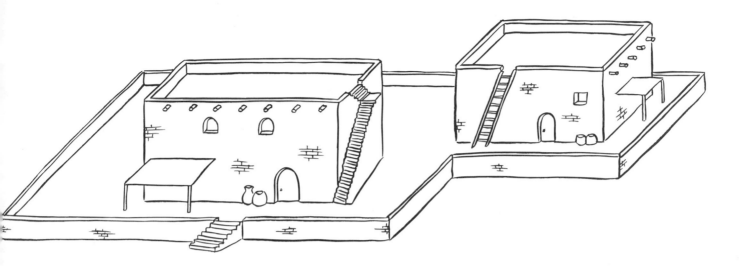

Bible Times Village

Modern Village

Goatskin Water Bottle

If you wish to make a life-size bottle, just enlarge these directions to whatever size you like. An actual goatskin bottle would be about two-feet-wide by three-feet-long, depending on the size of the goat.

Materials Needed:

- two 8½ inch by 12½ inch pieces of black felt
- string or twine
- hot glue gun
- scissors and chalk
- needle and thread (optional)
- ½ cup uncooked elbow macaroni, or other small pasta (optional)

Directions:

1. Using the pattern shown, make and cut out a stencil of the bottle.
2. Place the stencil on top of both pieces of felt. Trace the figure with chalk.
3. Cut out the figure from both pieces of felt.
4. Wipe off chalk marks with damp cloth
5. Apply hot glue along the interior lines, making sure not to glue along neck opening. Glue the pieces together. Let glue cool. (You can also sew the two halves together, but keep in mind that your stitches may have to be pretty tight to keep the contents of the bottle from falling out.)
6. Tightly tie off each of the four leg openings with string.
8. Fill the bottle with macaroni through the neck opening to give a "full bottle" effect. Tie the neck closed.
9. To make a strap for the goatskin bottle, tie three 36-inch-long pieces of twine together at one end. Then braid the three pieces together. When you are finished braiding, knot the other end. Attach the cord to the goatskin bottle either by tying each end to a leg or by sewing it on with needle and thread. (Ropes in the Middle East were commonly made from pieces of flax braided together and probably looked and felt a lot like this twine rope.)

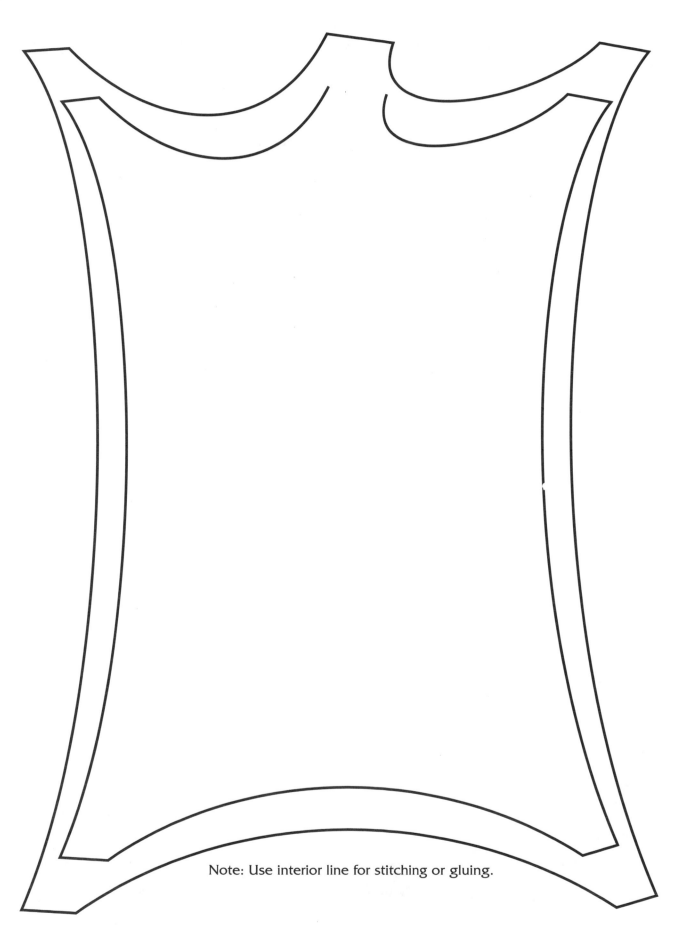

Note: Use interior line for stitching or gluing.

Road of the Roofs

Imgine you are one of Joshua's spies in Jericho. Try to find your way back to Rahab's roof near the wall. Remember, you cannot use the stairways or you will be caught.

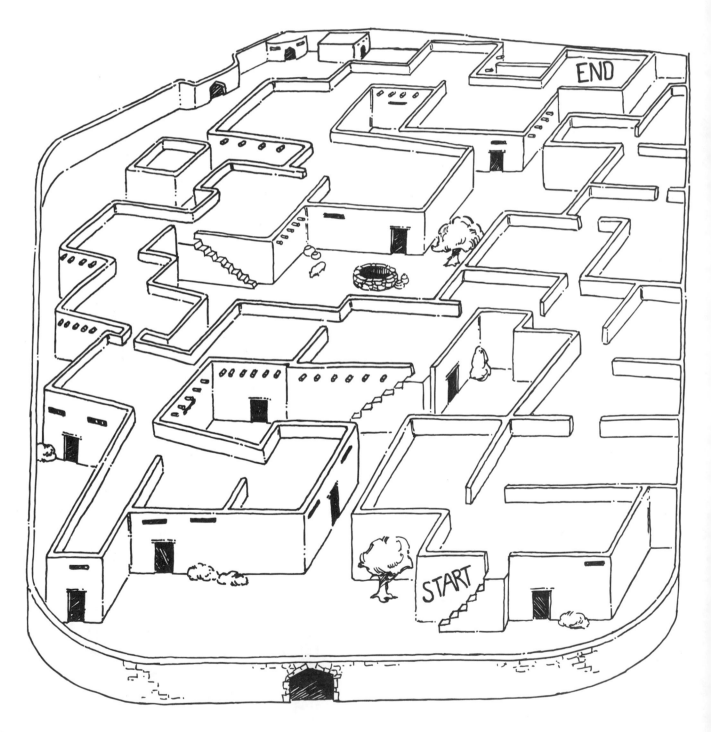

"Knocking at the Gate" Drama

In Bible times, guests did not simply knock on a wooden door with their knuckles; they called to their friends inside. The servant of the house would admit the guest only after he recognized the guest's voice. The following scene illustrates this custom.

Props:

• a gateway or closed door

Characters:

• Nicolas of Antioch (a visitor)
• Lutlas (a porter, or house servant)
• Timotheus (owner of the house)

Throughout the scene, Lutias is not visible; he is only heard. After he recognizes Nicolas' voice, the audience will see him.

(Nicolas taps on the gate with a stick.)

Lutias: Who's there?

Nicolas: It is I—peace be with you.

Lutias: Who comes to the door of my lord Timotheus?

Nicolas: It is a friend, come to bring peace and good news.

Lutias: Who is it? Who calls?

Nicolas: It is I, a weary traveler from Antioch.

Lutias (opening the door): Good friend, Nicolas! I recognize your voice at last! Come in, come in!

Welcome Game

The goal of this game is for the doorkeeper to let everyone in after recognizing his or her voice. To play the game, familiarize students with the "knocking at the gate" custom (see above).

Designate one child as doorkeeper. Have him stand behind a closed door, then introduce the first player. The first child calls to the doorkeeper. The doorkeeper has to identify the child by his call.

Give the doorkeeper three chances to see if he can identify the caller. If he can identify the caller by his voice, have the next child call, and so on. The child who is able to stump the doorkeeper becomes the next doorkeeper.

Chapter Two
Middle Eastern Cuisine

"And they, continuing daily with one accord in the temple, and breaking bread from house to house, did eat their meat with gladness and singleness of heart" (Acts 2:46).

"Wake up, Keriah. Time to grind grain."

It was early morning, and the rest of the household was asleep. Deborah, Keriah's mother, gently shook her daughter again. "Hurry and get dressed, daughter. We have much to do."

Eight-year-old Keriah stretched her arms over her head, then tossed off her covers and got up. She glanced at her five-year-old sister, Abigail, still asleep on a mat nearby. Keriah rolled up her mat and placed it in the corner. She slipped on her soft linen tunic, tied a blue sash around her waist, and joined her mother in the courtyard.

"The Passover is near, Keriah," her mother said as she bustled around the yard. "There is much to prepare. We'll grind barley grains first."

Keriah brought her mother a bowl of barley kernels. She sat cross-legged on the ground while her mother placed two heavy millstones in front of her. Deborah wedged a smaller bowl underneath the stones to catch the flour. Sitting opposite her daughter, Deborah poured the kernels into the funnel with one hand while rotating the heavy top stone with the other. Keriah helped her mother keep the top stone moving smoothly. Soon, a mound of beige flour filled the bowl.

"I'll start breakfast. Awaken your brother and sister," Deborah said. "Tell Micah I'll need more kindling. Be quick now, for the sun will soon be above the courtyard wall."

Keriah went into the one-room, brick house to awaken her little sister. She kissed her gently on the forehead.

"Wake up, sleepy lamb. Today is baking day."

Abigail opened her eyes and sat up. "Are we going with Uncle Andrew today?" she asked.

"Shhh! " Keriah whispered. She looked over her shoulder into the courtyard. Her mother was busy kneading the bread. "Let Micah ask. He'll know what to say."

Abigail rolled up her mat, placing

it in the corner next to Keriah's. Then she scrambled up the ladder to the loft.

"Micah! Micah! Are you asleep?" Abigail called. She climbed onto her brother's mat and shook him. "Are we going to with Uncle Andrew today? Are we going to see Jesus?"

Ten-year-old Micah laughed as he rubbed the sleep from his eyes. "Don't worry little lamb. We'll see Jesus today! But first you must let me get out of bed." Micah dressed quickly, slipping a small leather pouch into his belt. He climbed down the ladder with his little sister close behind. "Run and help mother, now, and leave the rest to me."

The girls stacked the flat barley loaves in a pile and placed a stone on top while their mother tended the clay oven. Micah strode in with a bundled of sticks in his arms. "This ought to do, Mother," he said, piling the sticks near the fire pit.

"Thank you, son. Now go and see to the oxen. Your father returns tomorrow, and I don't want him to find a dirty crib and starving animals," Deborah said.

"Yes, Mother—before I feed the animals, may I ask you something?" Micah asked. "Keriah and I would like to go someplace today."

"And me, too," Abigail added.

"Where, my son? Where will you go on baking day?"

"We'd like to go with Uncle Andrew," Keriah said.

"And where is my brother going today?" Deborah asked, looking up from her work.

"To see Jesus!" Abigail shouted. The three children immediately crowded around.

"He is the Messiah," Keriah said excitedly.

"Uncle Andrew says so!" Micah said.

"Everyone talks of the miracles Jesus does, Mother!" Keriah said.

"He healed multitudes in Jerusalem!" Micah added.

"Uncle says he healed the lame man at the sheep gate," Keriah said.

"And he healed a leopard, too, mama!" Abigail chimed in.

"Leper, Abigail," Micah corrected. "Yes, Mother. Uncle Andrew says it's true. He is going to see Jesus again today. Can we go with him, Mother. Please?"

"Please?" Keriah and Abigail begged.

"But what of my baking?" Deborah asked, flustered by the uproar.

"Can't Aunt Dinah help you?" Keriah offered. "She'll be here soon."

"Yes—that's true. But what about the oxen?"

"I'll clean the crib and put them to pasture on our way to Uncle's house," Micah said.

"But, who will watch over Abigail?"

"I will," Micah announced. "I always have my sling shot with me." He patted the leather pouch in his belt.

"Yes, Micah, so you do." Deborah said, resigned. "Oh, all right. You may go."

The three children cheered and hugged their mother.

"But take some food with you. If I know your uncle, you'll be gone all day." Deborah pulled down a small basket from a shelf and laid a coarse linen napkin inside. "Here are some barley loaves—five should do. And take these two salted fish as well." Deborah handed the basket to her son.

"Stay close by your uncle," Deborah said. "And by the wells of Jacob, Abigail, keep your veil on your head." Deborah tied her daughter's small blue veil tightly under her chin.

"I will, Mother," Abigail answered. "Shalom."

"Shalom!" she called to her children as they scurried out the door.

"Shalom, Mother! Shalom!"

Later that evening, Deborah heard her three children shouting in the streets.

"Mother! Mother! It's a miracle! A miracle!" Micah ran into the courtyard, breathless. His sisters were close behind.

"Jesus fed the multitude!" Keriah shouted.

"With our fish and bread!" said Abigail.

"What? How? I gave you only a few fish and five loaves!" Deborah said, astonished.

"Wait until we tell you what happened," Micah said. All three children talked at once.

"Jesus taught us all day."

"And after that, everyone was so hungry. There were so many people, but no food."

"Then Uncle Andrew told Jesus about Micah's basket with the five loaves and two fish."

"And I gave him the fish and bread, and Jesus fed everyone!"

"And there were twelve baskets left over."

"It's a miracle!" shouted Abigail. And she tossed her veil in the air for joy.

Middle Eastern Cuisine

In the lands and times of the Bible, women prepared the food for their families, from grinding grain to churning butter to drying grapes and figs. One of the first things a woman did early each day was to bake enough bread for her household, including any servants she employed (see Proverbs 31:15). After her morning bath and prayers, she lit a fire in the courtyard, then ground grain in a stone flour mill.

To grind grain, two women sat cross-legged facing one another with two large, flat stones about eighteen inches in diameter positioned between them. The women then took turns rotating the top stone over the bottom while steadily pouring kernels into the top. (The top stone had a handle on it and an opening in which to pour grain.) To the Middle Easterner, the sound of grinding grain is a pleasant sound, associated with home, comfort, and plenty. In describing pending desolation, the prophet Jeremiah said, "I will take from them the voice of mirth, and the voice of gladness. . . the sound of the millstones" (Jeremiah 25:10). After grinding the flour and preparing the dough, the woman baked a day's worth of bread either directly on the hearth or in an oven. Along with the fresh barley loaves, a woman might serve her family a breakfast of olives, cheese, and warm goat's milk.

Besides bread, the ancient Near Eastern diet was simple: fresh fruits and vegetables, legumes, nuts, seeds, grains like wheat and barley, honey, goat's milk, and on occasion, some meat and fish. Medical archaeologists have discovered that ancient Egyptians ate apples, barley, garlic, leeks, lentils, melons, onions, radishes, seeds, and wheat. In addition, the Israelites followed the strict dietary guidelines from the Torah.

Reclining to Eat

Tent dwelling families probably ate their meals sitting on a rug spread on the ground. But by the Gospel period, the popular custom was to eat in a semi-reclining position propped up on pillows. Diners were usually arranged around a U-shaped table to allow ease of service. A large pot of food called the common bowl was placed in the center of the table, and each person could reach in to dip his or her bread.

Just as they did in ancient times, Middle Eastern people today usually eat with their hands and not with a fork or spoon. They use a piece of bread like we use utensils, scooping up morsels of food or dipping bread in soups and stews. "What does a man want of a spoon when God has given him so many fingers?" asks an Arabian proverb. Because Middle Eastern people don't use utensils, hand washing was an essential part of every meal. Before food was served, a servant would pour water over each family member's hands before they sat down to eat. A prayer of thanks was given, perhaps this traditional meal-time prayer: "Blessed art thou, Jehovah our God, King of the world, who causes to come forth bread from the earth."

Search the Scriptures

Being a disciple in the lands and times of the Bible meant doing mundane tasks for the master, such as serving table or washing feet and hands. As a sign that a disciple's training was complete, he would pour water on his master's hands. Some say that when Elisha poured water on Elijah, this indicated his competency to be a prophet (2 Kings 3:11).

Romans 12:20 speaks of heaping coals of fire on someone's head. Early in the morning, a boy would carry coals from house to house so that others could start their morning fires. He carried the hot coals in a potsherd on his head. (See Pillai's book LIGHT THROUGH AN EASTERN WINDOW, pages 112 and 113.) This was a pleasant task, for it warmed the boy as he, in turn, helped others. The inference here is to repay evil with good, and not to seek vengeance.

One type of hand grindstone found in the Ha'aretz Museum in Tel Aviv

Bread of Life

Bread is a staple in the Middle East, both ancient and modern. To the Middle Eastern mind, bread is sacred—parents teach their children that bread gives them life. Middle Eastern people almost always break bread rather than cut it, because to them, slicing bread is like cutting life itself. The expressions "to break bread" or to "eat bread" became synonymous for eating a meal. For instance, when Jesus Christ instructed his disciples to pray for "daily bread," they would have understood that he meant a daily provision of food (Luke 11:3).

We know that bread was a staple food in the Bible lands, but what did the loaves look like, and how were they cooked? Basically, bread came in two forms, leavened and unleavened, and was generally made from wheat, barley, rye, or spelt flour. If loaves were leavened (from the Latin word *levare* meaning "to raise"), they contained a leavening agent, such as yeast or fermented dough (sourdough). This type of loaf took considerable time to make, for the dough had to rise before being baked. The result was a light, soft loaf.

In contrast, unleavened bread was quick to make and came out thin, flat, and chewy. The familiar Mexican tortilla or Indian *chapati* are two types of unleavened bread eaten today. (Keep in mind that not all flat bread is unleavened, though. Pita bread contains yeast and is therefore leavened bread.) Scholars say that this disc-shaped, unleavened bread is the common bread of the Bible—flat enough to be mistaken for a stone (see Matthew 7:9) and pliable enough to be tucked away for travel.

When it came to baking, women in the ancient Near East had a variety of options. They could lay dough directly on heated stones or hot coals, one of the most primitive methods of baking. Bread could also be cooked on a large, earthenware jug called a clay oven. Wood or dung burned underneath or inside one of these jars, making the surface piping hot. Visitors to the Bible lands say that women throughout the Middle East still cook on this type of clay oven. Women might also bake their loaves in public ovens where they shared the task with others. Like meeting at the well for water, this gathering at the ovens was a time of pleasant fellowship for the hard-working women of the Middle East. Large cities might have several public ovens, and bakeries too, where baked goods were sold. Jerusalem had a baker's street in Jeremiah's day (Jeremiah 37:21).

Land of milk and honey

Next to bread, the most important and versatile food in the ancient Near East was milk. Because clean drinking water was scarce and wells were jealously guarded, people relied on goat's milk to quench their thirst. Milk could also be made into cheese, butter,

yogurt, and *leben*, a fermented beverage still drunk by Arabs today. Meaning "white," leben is made by sprinkling yeast into fresh milk and letting it stand. Leben keeps for several days and was commonly carried in goatskin bottles whenever water wasn't available.

In biblical times, butter was churned inside goatskin bottles. After filling the skin with milk, the bottle was tightly tied and then suspended from a wooden tripod. The women in the household then took turns rocking, kneading, and shaking the bottle back and forth until the milk thickened. This could take all day. Cheese was made about the same way with salt added later as a preservative. Once molded into cakes, the cheese was covered with a cloth, and a heavy stone was placed on top to squeeze out excess water.

To satisfy a sweet tooth, people of the Bible lands ate fruit, such as figs, grapes, raisins, and pomegranates, and cakes sweetened with grape juice syrup or honey. Historians say that the Palestine area, described in the Bible as a land "flowing with milk and honey," once produced an abundance of the sticky, golden liquid. The Bible compares several things to this unique food: the judgment of God's Word (see Psalm 19:10), pleasant words (see Proverbs 16:24), and knowledge and wisdom (see Proverbs 24:13, 14). Honeycomb was a favorite treat in the ancient Near East—one of the few things Jesus Christ ate after he was resurrected (Luke 24:42, 43).

Search the Scriptures

After a woman baked bread, she would stack the brown discs into a pile, placing a smooth stone on top to keep them warm. A person might mistake one of these flat stones for a piece of flat, brown bread (Matthew 7:9-11). While a father might mistakenly hand his son a stone in place of bread, God would never give his children anything less than "good things to them that ask."

The expression "a land flowing with milk and honey" is a figurative term meaning that the land would produce abundantly, having a rich store of honey and verdant pastures capable of sustaining many livestock. To a predominantly agricultural community, this expression would have communicated physical abundance.

Proverbs 30:33 compares churning milk and wringing the nose to forcing wrath because the outcomes of these three activities are certain. Because churning milk into butter was universal in the ancient Near East, this comparison would have been understood by nearly everyone.

Seasoned With Salt

Numerous herbs and spices are mentioned in the Bible such as myrrh, cinnamon, and saffron, but undoubtedly the most versatile and important spice used in the Middle East was salt. In addition to preserving and flavoring food, salt could be used as an antiseptic to cleanse wounds. Metaphorically, salt represented loyalty and fidelity. This spice was also used in the ancient custom of salting and swaddling infants (see Chapter 5) and in the salt covenant.

Considered to be the highest of all ancient pledges, the salt covenant is an outward sign of fidelity. If two people ate a salted meal together, they were agreeing never to betray one another, even at the risk of death. To the Middle Eastern mind, nothing could break this vow (Numbers 18:19). Salt covenants might be exchanged between master and servant, husband and wife, or guest and protector. David's kingdom was sealed with a salt covenant: "Ought ye not to know that the Lord God of Israel gave the kingdom over Israel to David for ever, even to him and to his sons by a covenant of salt?" (2 Chronicles 13:5).

Another type of grindstone with upper and lower stones (Ha'aretz Museum, Tel Aviv)

Curious Cuisine

Some of the fascinating foodstuff mentioned in the Bible include the lump of figs used to cure Hezekiah's boil (2 Kings 20:7), the pulse that Daniel ate (Daniel 1:12), and John the Baptist's meal of wild honey and locusts (Matthew 3:4). Scientists say that figs contain a cancer-fighting chemical called benzaldehyde, a proven remedy for malignant tumors. Bible scholars believe that the pulse Daniel and his friends ate probably were lentils, because the Hebrew word translated "pulse" means "something that is sown or planted." And about those locusts that John the Baptist ate, they may have been carob bean pods, as well as crunchy insects. In the Middle East, locust refers not only to insects but also to carob, a tree that grows throughout the Bible lands. This tree produces edible pods commonly used as fodder, although the insects called locusts were considered clean cuisine according to Old Testament Law (Leviticus 11:22).

In the lands and times of the Bible, people ate simple foods: fruits and vegetables, whole grains, nuts, seeds, and legumes. They drank goat's milk and wine and ate meat and fish on occasion. In addition, the Israelites followed strict dietary guidelines from the Law. Although they did not have modern conveniences like stoves, refrigerators, or even running water, people in the ancient Near East thrived on a very simple diet—similar to those recommended by many health organizations today.

Search the Scriptures

In the Middle East salt is stored in large stone jars kept in the kitchen where every day the floor is washed with water. Over time, the base of the jar becomes soaked with water, and the salt at the bottom loses some of its saltiness. When a person reaches this useless salt, he throws it out into the street where it is walked on. Jesus was likely referring to this custom in Matthew 5:13.

The sayings "Have salt in yourselves" (Mark 9:50) and "Let your speech be always with grace, seasoned with salt" (Colossians 4:6) refer to the importance of having integrity of speech—meaning what you say and saying what you mean. Salt was symbolic in the ancient Near East for loyalty, faithfulness, and integrity.

Simple Traditional Seder Plate

Seder is the ceremonial dinner usually held on the first night of the Passover celebration. There are many variations of recipes and traditions of what is served with the "traditional" seder meal, but here is a simple variation that you can use in a classroom setting.

Many Jewish families have a special seder plate, a large, ornate plate with a place for each of the traditional symbols of the Passover: bitter herbs, vegetable, haroset, shankbone of a lamb, and a roasted egg.

The bitter herbs symbolize the bitterness of the nation of Israel's slavery in Egypt. They are often represented by horseradish. You can find fresh horseradish in the produce section of many grocery stores and prepared horseradish in the refrigerated foods section.

Parsley is often used as the vegetable and is usually dipped in salt water at the seder. The salt water is said to symbolize the tears of the Hebrew slaves in Egypt, and the leafy parsley is often said to represent the hyssop that was used to mark the doorposts and lintel with the blood of the Passover lamb.

Haroset, while not a biblical part of the first Passover meal, is a traditional part of the seder meal. It is usually a mixture of chopped apples, raisins, figs, and walnuts, and it represents the mortar used by the Hebrew slaves to build monuments and walls for the Egyptians. An easy-to-make version of haroset is a mixture of applesauce, raisins, and chopped walnuts.

The shankbone of the lamb is the centerpiece of the seder plate, as the lamb is the centerpiece of the first Passover. (Some may say, "There is no deliverance without the blood of the lamb.") You may have to visit a butcher to get a shankbone without actually serving lamb.

Many Jewish seder plates feature a roasted egg to symbolize the sacrifice of a lamb in addition to the lamb eaten for the Passover meal. This may also be a symbol of spring, the season of Passover, and for this reason you can make a connection to the typically secular tradition of hard-boiled Easter eggs.

While not part of the traditional seder plate, unleavened bread was a vital part of the Passover meal instituted in Exodus 12. The Passover lamb was to be eaten with unleavened bread and bitter herbs (Numbers 9:11). Many Christians today use unleavened bread in their celebration of the Lord's Supper.

There are specific seder readings and traditions that have a ritual for filling glasses and drinking wine throughout the meal. Again, wine has a central role in the Last Supper and in the Communion traditions of the modern church. While scholars may argue over whether it is appropriate to use wine or grape juice, it is certainly preferable to use grape juice in classroom seder, Passover, or Lord's Supper applications.

Traditional clay vessels for a typical
Middle Eastern "table" setting

Dibs

Ingredients:
- White grape juice
- Heavy duty pan

Directions:
Bring the juice to a boil and continue boiling until enough water has evaporated to leave a thick paste. Tent dwellers spread this sweet, sticky substance on bread. Some use it like honey in their cooking.

Raisins

Ingredients:
- 2 or 3 pounds of grapes (white, purple, or red)
- 2 to 4 teaspoons olive oil
- Heavy string (optional)
- Baking sheets

Directions:
1. Remove the grapes from their stems, and wash and dry them thoroughly.
2. Spread the grapes on the baking sheets and brush them lightly with olive oil.
3. Set the pans in the hot summer sun, flipping them every day until they are dried.

Another way to dry grapes is to string the bunches of grapes on heavy string. Brush them lightly with olive oil and hang them in the sun until they dry.

You may want to try both methods to see which works faster or more effectively.

Unleavened Bread

Ingredients:

- 4 cups flour
- 1 teaspoon oil
- large mixing bowl
- iron skillet or frying pan
- 2 cups water
- pinch of salt
- rolling pin
- spatula

Directions:

1. Mix the flour and salt. Slowly add oil and water. Knead the dough until it is soft and elastic, but not too wet. Cover and let stand for 5 minutes.
2. Pre-heat the skillet on medium heat. (It is important that you not bake the bread on high heat.)
3. Coat your hands and workspace with some flour to prevent sticking. Break off a small amount of dough, about the size of a golf ball. Coat the ball with some flour and then flatten it with the palm of your hand.
4. Roll out the dough until it is a circle 6 inches in diameter, about the size of a bread plate. (Don't press too hard while rolling the dough, or it will stick.)
5. Shake the excess flour from the dough by flipping the dough from one hand to the other. This will also stretch the dough a little more.
6. Place the bread onto the heated pan and bake it until it begins to bubble or puff up a bit. Flip the bread over and bake the other side. Both sides should be uniform in color, so you may have to flip it a few times to bake it evenly.

Ezekiel Bread

Ingredients:

- 4 packets of yeast
- 8 cups wheat flour
- 2 cups soy flour
- 1 cup lentils, cooked and mashed
- 4 to 5 tablespoons olive oil
- 1 cup warm water
- 4 cups barley flour
- ½ cup millet flour
- ⅓ to ½ cup honey
- 4 cups water
- 1 tablespoon salt

Directions:

1. Dissolve yeast in 1 cup warm water and 1 tablespoon honey. Set aside for 10 minutes.
2. Combine the different flours.
3. Blend lentils, oil, remaining honey, and a small amount of water in a blender. Place in a large bowl with remaining water.
4. Stir in two cups of mixed flour.
5. Add the yeast mixture. Stir in the remaining salt and flour.
6. Knead until smooth. Put the dough in an oiled bowl and let it rise until double in size.
7. Knead again and cut and shape dough into four loaves. Place loaves in greased pans. Let them rise until the top is just over the edge of the pans.
8. Bake at 375 degrees Fahrenheit for 45 to 60 minutes.

Shishlik
(Lamb Skewers)

This is a popular, yet ancient, method of cooking meat. The traditions for shishlik are found all over the Middle East and throughout the Mediterranean regions.

Ingredients:

- 1 pound tender lamb (or beef)
- 1 clove garlic, crushed
- 1 tablespoon olive oil
- salt and pepper to taste

Directions:

1. Cut the meat into cubes or strips.
2. Make a marinade with the olive oil and garlic, and marinate the meat for about 45 minutes.
3. Run skewers through the meat and place skewers over a charcoal fire. (You could also broil the skewers in an oven.) Salt and pepper to taste.

Hummus

Hummus, or chick-pea dip, is a popular appetizer of the Middle East and Mediterranean region. It is often served with fresh bread.

Ingredients:

- 2 cups canned chick peas, drained
- ¼ cup fresh squeezed lemon juice or the juice of 2 lemons
- 1 teaspoon salt
- ¼ teaspoon cumin
- 3 tablespoons pure tahini paste (optional)
- 2 cloves garlic, crushed
- 2 to 3 tablespoons olive oil

Directions:

1. Place all the ingredients in a blender or a food processor and puree until chick peas are smooth.
2. Serve well chilled with pita bread or crackers. (Hummus ought to be stored in a covered container.)

Esau's Pottage
(Lentil Stew)

Ingredients:

- 1 medium onion, chopped
- 1 tablespoon olive oil
- ½ teaspoon ground cumin
- ½ teaspoon coriander
- 2 cloves garlic, minced
- 1 cup lentils
- 3 cups beef stock
- salt to taste

Directions:

1. Sauté the chopped onion, cumin, and coriander in olive oil in a large pot. As the onion softens, add the minced garlic and sauté until browned.
2. Add the beef stock and lentils and bring to a boil. When the stock begins to boil, reduce the heat to simmer.
3. When the lentils are tender, about 45 to 60 minutes, salt to taste and serve.

Mango Lassi

This recipe is actually from India. It is similar to the traditional Arabic drink leben but doesn't include warm, fermented goat's milk, which might be unpleasant for children.

Directions:

On slow speed, blend all ingredients together in blender, adding the honey or sugar to taste.

Ingredients:

- 2 cups plain yogurt
- ½ to 1 cup water
- mango pulp (or another fruit)
- honey (or sugar to taste)

Sourdough Bread Starter

Ingredients:

- 1 tablespoon yeast
- 2 cups warm water
- 2 cups flour

Directions:

1. In a glass container, dissolve yeast in water. Let stand 10 minutes.
2. Stir in the flour. Cover and let stand in a warm place overnight or at room temperature for about two days or until the mixture is bubbly and sour smelling. (If you like your bread to taste more sour, you can let it stand longer.)

The starter is now ready to use, but you must store the remainder in a closed container in the refrigerator. When you use more starter, stir in equal amounts of warm water and flour to the original and let it stand again until it is bubbly. Stir the starter before storing it. If the starter gets too sour, discard 1 cup and add 1 cup warm water and 1 cup flour and then let it stand again. The starter should last indefinitely if it is used at least once a week.

Sourdough Bread

Ingredients:

- 2 cups sourdough starter
- 1 cup milk
- ¼ cup butter
- ¼ cup sugar or honey
- 2 teaspoons salt
- 2 teaspoons baking soda
- 5 to 7 cups flour

Directions:

1. Heat the milk until it is scalding hot.
2. Stir the butter, sugar, and salt into the heated milk and cool the mixture until lukewarm.
3. Add the sourdough starter, soda, and a little warm water and stir.
4. Add flour until it is kneadable. Knead the dough well. Let the dough rise four about 3 hours.
5. When the dough has doubled in volume, punch it down and form two loaves.
6. Place the loaves in greased loaf pans and let the dough rise until it is just above the edge of the pans.
7. Bake at 400 degrees Fahrenheit for 25 to 30 minutes.

Kebob

Not to be confused with shishlik, kebob is a classic Middle Eastern dish that resembles hamburgers.

Ingredients:

- 2 pounds ground lamb (or beef)
- ½ to 1 teaspoon ground cumin
- ¼ cup chopped parsley (to taste)
- ½ cup water
- medium to large onion
- salt and pepper (to taste)

Directions:

1. Mix the ground lamb with the cumin, salt, and pepper.
2. Add the water slowly until the mixture is just a bit less solid than it was to begin with, but not so wet that it falls through the grill.
3. Chop the onion and add it with the chopped parsley to the mixture.
4. Form the mixture into a large loaf and let it sit in the refrigerator overnight to let the flavors mingle.
5. Prior to grilling the kebobs, form small sausage-link-like burgers (about 3 inches long).
6. Grill for about 6 minutes, or until browned.

Middle Eastern Salad

This salad is more Mediterranean than Middle Eastern, but it is a modern staple in Israel, often eaten with every meal of the day.

Ingredients:

- ½ head lettuce
- ¼ head cabbage
- 3 to 4 medium tomatoes
- 2 medium cucumbers
- 1 large carrot
- 6 to 12 radishes
- 2 or 3 green onions
- 2 medium hard-boiled eggs
- chopped parsley (to taste)
- 2 to 3 tablespoons lemon juice
- 2 to 3 tablespoons olive oil

Directions:

1. Break up the lettuce into bite-size pieces by hand.
2. Chop all the vegetables into small pieces. (You may want to grate the carrot instead.)
3. Grate the hard-boiled eggs and mix all the ingredients well with equal amounts of lemon juice and olive oil. (If you won't be serving the salad soon after making it, wait to add the lemon juice and olive oil dressing until immediately before serving.)

Moussaka

Although Moussaka is a traditional Greek dish, it has found its way into a number of Mediterranean and Middle Eastern cuisines.

Ingredients:

- 2 large eggplants
- 4 medium eggs
- 2 tablespoons flour
- 2 cups water or vegetable stock
- 2 tablespoons olive oil
- 1 pound ground lamb
- 1 large onion
- 2 medium tomatoes
- 2 cloves garlic (minced)
- salt (to taste)

Directions

1. Wash and dry the eggplants and cut into rings. Sprinkle the rings with salt and let stand for about an hour.
2. Chop the onion and fry in olive oil until it begins to turn soft.
3. Add the lamb and garlic and fry until slightly browned.
4. Chop the tomatoes and add to the mixture. Simmer for about 15 minutes. Then set the mixture aside.
5. Coat the eggplant rings lightly with flour and fry in olive oil until slightly browned.
6. Place the fried rings in a casserole dish, layering the rings with the meat mixture.
7. Bake covered at 325 degrees Fahrenheit for 40 to 45 minutes.
8. Stir about 2 teaspoons of cornstarch into the stock and add the slightly beaten eggs. Pour the egg mixture over the casserole.
9. Bake at 350 degrees Fahrenheit until the egg and stock mixture begins to be absorbed.

Chicken Souvlaki

This traditional Greek dish is similar to shishlik and probably comes closer to what many people will call shish kabobs.

Ingredients:

- ½ cup olive oil
- ¼ cup lemon juice
- ¼ cup red wine vinegar
- 1 clove garlic, minced
- 1 tablespoon oregano
- 1½ to 2 pounds boneless chicken breast
- 2 medium green bell peppers
- 1 to 1½ pounds whole mushrooms

Directions:

1. Cut the chicken breast into 1-inch cubes.
2. Combine all other ingredients to make a marinade.
3. Soak the chicken breast in the marinade for about three or four hours.
4. Clean the peppers and cut them into 1-inch square pieces.
5. Run skewers through alternating pieces of chicken, peppers, and mushrooms until all the pieces of meat and vegetables are used up.
6. Grill the skewered meat and vegetables for about 15-20 minutes, occasionally brushing with leftover marinade.

Additional Activities

1. Purchase some wheat berries at a health food store, and try to grind them into flour. You can use a mortar and pestle, a hand flour mill (try kitchen stores), or a food processor. This will give you some idea of the time it took to grind and bake bread daily. Note: the result will be coarse meal, not the fine texture of refined white flour.

2. Taste some honeycomb—you can buy it in a health food store. Compare it to other sweet things, such as barley malt, sugar, or maple syrup. If you can find it, try wild honey. Wild honey has not been pasteurized. It can be purchased in most health food stores and in many groceries. (Check to make sure that the honey you give to young children is pasteurized. Some doctors recommend not giving honey to children younger than a year old.)

3. Using a sturdy plastic bag—the kind that seals tight—try churning milk into butter. (Hint: use warm milk with a ½ teaspoon of sugar added.) This will give you some idea how long it took to churn butter. Note: the goal is to solidify the milk, not produce a perfect slab of butter like you'd get at a grocery store. This will take some time.

4. From the Old Testament, make list all the clean and unclean foods. For older students, study what makes some unclean foods unhealthy. For example, according to Leviticus 7:23, 24, fat was to be trimmed off meats. Today, we know that impurities are stored in animal fats. Additionally, animal fats are high in unhealthy saturated fats, whereas vegetable fats are preferred. For teachers: you can have students draw or cut out pictures of animals, then have them place them on either side of these headings: "clean" and "unclean" foods.

5. Study Old Testament cooking laws—how do they ensure health and sanitation?

6. Study the New Testament to see what dietary wisdom exists today.

Chapter Three

Middle Eastern Dress Code

"But what went ye out for to see? A man clothed in soft raiment? Behold, they that wear soft clothing are in kings' houses" (Matthew 11:8).

The market at Jericho was unusually busy. Traders from Damascus had just unloaded their boats filled with merchandise—brass lamps, pottery, leather goods, sparkling jewels, and baskets full of silk, wool, and linen. Amidst the hubbub, Benjamin the tailor sat at his booth quietly assessing his new merchandise.

"This Egyptian cotton is magnificent," he muttered to himself as he ran his bony fingers down the bolt of silky blue fabric. "It would make a lovely tunic for my little Sarah. But first, I must finish this garment for the tetrarch." Reluctantly, the old man put aside the silken fabric and took up a cloak that lay in a heap by his side. Metal needle in hand, Benjamin hemmed the garment with quick, even stitches. He was engrossed in his work when a man approached.

"You there, tailor. Let me see some of that scarlet wool from Damascus," the man said, pointing to a bolt of fabric behind the tailor. He was a short man, and Benjamin thought he might be an errand boy. But something urgent in the man's voice and the glint in his eye told Benjamin otherwise.

"For you, or for your master?" Benjamin teased.

"For me, you silly fool, " the man snapped. "Be quick about it. I must be at receipt of customs by noon."

Benjamin spread out the heavy red fabric in front of the man. He stooped down to examine the cloth. Benjamin took up his needle again. *His tunic is fine linen, I see—seamless, too!* Benjamin thought. *The delicate gold stitching around the cuffs, exquisite. He must be rich. And that purple girdle belongs to no beggar, I'm sure. That pouch on his belt looks full enough. I wonder where he earns his silver?*

"This will do," the diminutive man said, snapping Benjamin out of his reverie. "I want you to make a robe out of this, embroidered with gold and lined with silk. Can you do it?"

"Can you pay for it?" Benjamin asked.

"Yes, of course. Don't you know who I am?"

"Should I?"

"If you pay your taxes you should."

Benjamin glared at the man. "Your heavy purse betrays you—you are a tax collector?"

"*Chief* tax collector. And my purse is earned honestly, tailor."

"By extortion you mean. You publicans are wolves—the lot of you."

"Is this any way to talk to a paying customer? Besides, if I accidentally take more than I should, I pay it back fourfold."

"But you squeeze us dry like an empty goatskin only to feed that Roman pig, the emperor." Benjamin spat on the ground. "He grows fat while the poor beg for crusts in the streets. And it's all at your hands, chief publican."

"I give to the poor. What more can I do?"

Benjamin's answer was drowned out by loud noises coming from outside the city gate. A large crowd streamed into the marketplace—men, women, and children. A few were on donkeys, but most were walking. They followed a Judean man dressed in a coarse linen robe.

"It's the rabbi, Jesus of Nazareth!" the publican exclaimed.

"Some say he healed a blind man in Jerusalem. Do you believe it, tax collector?" Benjamin asked. But it was too late. The little man was running across the marketplace towards the crowd.

"Wait! I didn't measure you!" Benjamin called after him. He watched as the small figure reached the multitude and tried, in vain, to push through to the rabbi. The little man stood on tiptoes, trying to see past the throng; but it was no use. Then he did something that made Benjamin shake with laughter. The tax collector ran to a nearby fig tree and scaled its branches. There, from his perch above the crowds, Zacchaeus could see everything.

Middle Eastern Clothing

While we might have a closet filled with shirts, pants, and shoes, the average person in Bible times had only one change of clothes and the sandals on his feet. In the ancient Near East, clothes were a costly commodity. It could take days or weeks to make one garment—from spinning thread, to dying cloth, to sewing the pieces together by hand. Because of its worth, clothing was often exchanged for goods in place of money or given as gifts. For example, Joseph gave his brothers "changes of raiment" to celebrate their reunion (Genesis 45:22), and Naaman considered "ten changes of raiment" a gift fit for a king (2 Kings 5:5). Aside from its monetary value, clothing also reflected a person's position in society, or in some instances, his emotional state.

In Bible times, a woman made nearly all the clothing for her household. She used soft fabrics like cotton and linen (made from flax plants) to make fine garments, and wool and leather (made from sheep, goat, or camel hides) to fashion sturdier, outer tunics. Making clothes was no simple task. To make a woolen coat, the woman first spun raw wool into thread. Using a handloom, she then wove the threads into cloth and dyed the fabric with homemade tints derived from flowers, plants, or other organic materials. Finally, she sewed the pieces together using a brass or bone needle. It's no wonder that in biblical times, a woman was considered wise and virtuous if she was able to clothe her family well (see Proverbs 31:13, 19, 21, 22 and Exodus 35:25, 26).

But what about the average person? What were his everyday clothes like? Historians say that people in Bible times normally wore three garments: an under tunic, an outer tunic, and a cloak. They strapped sandals on their feet (or went barefooted) and wrapped a covering around their heads. Men and women wore similarly styled garments, only women's tunics were longer and more decorative.

If the ancient Near Easterner did not wear a loincloth, a simple piece of cloth wrapped or fastened around the waist, the first thing he put on was his under tunic. This lightweight garment hung to the knees and looked like a large, sleeveless shirt with no collar. In warm weather, this was all the clothing a child would wear. Before retiring at night, the ancient Near Easterner would strip down to his under tunic, what he considers to be his underwear. Over this came the heavier coat—knee length for a man and ankle length for a woman.

In colder weather, the Near Easterner donned a third garment called a cloak—a thick, long-sleeved robe usually made from animal skins or dense wool. Travelers and shepherds would almost always wear a cloak, for it could double as their bed and blanket at night (see Exodus 22:26, 27 and Deuteronomy 24:13). Tunics opened in front and were tied together with a belt, also called a "girdle" in the Bible.

When we think of a girdle, we might picture a tight-fitting corset worn around the waist or hips, but in biblical culture, a girdle was a wide strip of cloth that was wrapped several times around the midriff. Middle Easterners like to carry small items like daggers, money, or a shepherd's purse in the folds of these belts. A scribe could slip his small ink case into his girdle (see Ezekiel 9:2-3), and a shepherd might tuck a lamb into his belt folds in order to carry the animal to safety.

Occasionally, men would wear a fourth garment called a "mantle." When the Bible mentions a mantle, it's referring to a thick piece of fabric worn around the shoulders, similar to a woman's stole or shawl. Often in ancient religions, a mantle was placed on the shoulders of young men when they are called to religious service. Evidently this custom existed in Old Testament times: "So he departed thence, and found Elisha the son of Shaphat, who was plowing with twelve yoke of oxen before him, and he with the twelfth: and Elijah passed by him, and cast his mantle upon him" (1 Kings 19:19). This transference symbolized Elisha's succession as prophet.

Clothed in Purple

We might think that apparel in biblical times was drab, but historians say that clothing came in a rainbow of colors. In New Testament times, for example, women commonly wore blue. Yellow, red, indigo, black, and purple cloth was also available throughout the ancient Near East. The crocus flower produced yellow dye; the indigo plant, blue. Purple, which was the most expensive tint in the ancient world, came from a sea snail. (It takes about 60,000 shells to make just one pound of dye!) Making and selling dye was usually women's work. Lydia, who is mentioned in the book of Acts, sold this vibrant pigment (Acts 16:14).

In many ancient cultures, the color of clothing was not so much an expression of personal style as it was an indication of someone's station in society. For instance, if a boy in New Testament times wore a purple-striped garment, that meant he was freeborn. Victorious generals and emperors paraded in cloaks hemmed in purple and gold. Royalty usually wore purple, blue, and scarlet, while mourners wore black.

Search the Scriptures

Considering the value of clothing in Old Testament times, when Samson offered thirty shirts and thirty changes of clothing as a prize for solving his riddle, he was offering a small fortune! (See Judges 14:12.)

The phrase "gird up your loins" is mentioned throughout the Bible. In ancient times, if a person wanted to run without tripping over his garments, he would pull his tunic up between his legs and tuck it into his belt. To "gird the loins," therefore, became a metaphor for being prepared. When God commanded the Israelites to eat the Passover with their "loins girded," it meant that they should be ready to leave Egypt (Exodus 12:11).

Sackcloth and Ashes

Search the Scriptures

John the Baptist wore "raiment of camel's hair, and a leathern girdle about his loins" (Matthew 3:4). Even though he wore sackcloth, John the Baptist was not in mourning. Bible scholars say that John wore coarse material as a sign of his submission to God and a leather girdle instead of a soft linen one to show that he was not looking for a life of luxury or comfort. To the Near Eastern mind, John the Baptist's clothing was a sign of his devotion to God.

In the ancient Near East, ripping or tearing a mantle or other garment symbolized profound anger or grief. Because of the value of clothing, to tear a garment would be shocking. When Ezra the scribe tore both his garment (tunic) and his mantle, people would have understood the gravity of the situation (Ezra 9:3).

Not only would the color of his clothes reflect a person's societal status, so would the type and texture of his fabric. Commoners wore coarse linen or wool while wealthy people draped themselves in silk and a finer grade of linen. Sometimes the type of fabric bespoke a person's inner state, too. For instance, Bible times people dressed in sackcloth and smeared their faces with ashes when they were in deep distress or in mourning. Sackcloth, a coarse material made from either camel or goat's hair, is similar to burlap; the rough, scratchy texture irritates the skin. When Jacob thought his beloved son, Joseph, had been killed, he "rent his clothes, and put sackcloth upon his loins, and mourned for his son many days" (Genesis 37:34). A person might also wear sackcloth while fasting (Daniel 9:3) or to signify his devotion to God.

Coat of Many Colors

One well-known robe mentioned in the Bible is Joseph's coat of many colors. Some Bible scholars say that Joseph's coat was special, not because it was multicolored, but because it was made with long sleeves (the Hebrew word for "color" can also be translated "pieces"). Such coats were reserved for the family's heir. In the ancient Near East, a man's inheritance normally went to his oldest son, and in Israel's family, that would have been Reuben. Therefore, Joseph's robe was not just a present from a loving father—it was a sign that Joseph was to be Israel's heir (see Genesis 37).

Another famous robe is the seamless one belonging to Jesus Christ (John 19:23, 24). Historians tell us that this type of cloak had to be of the very latest style, for looms capable of weaving seamless garments were only invented in Jesus' day. Coats woven from one piece of cloth were rare and thereby more costly than coats with seams. The soldiers didn't tear Jesus' robe because they doubtless knew its value. Yet, this garment holds added significance, considering that, according to the ancient historian Josephus, only high priests wore seamless tunics. This takes on added meaning in light of verses such as Hebrews 3:1: "Wherefore, holy brethren, partakers of the heavenly calling, consider the Apostle and High Priest of our profession, Christ Jesus."

Search the Scriptures

To dress someone in fine linen meant you were honoring him. For example, when Pharaoh elevated Joseph to second in his kingdom, he "arrayed him in vestures of fine linen, and put a gold chain about his neck" (Genesis 41:42). When the king honored Mordecai, he dressed Mordecai in "royal apparel of blue and white, and with a great crown of gold, and with a garment of fine linen and purple" (Esther 8:15). As a gesture of love and respect, Joseph of Aramithea wrapped the dead body of Jesus Christ in fine linen (Mark 15:46).

In ancient lands, the colors red, blue, and purple were associated with royalty. The Roman soldiers dressed Jesus Christ in a scarlet robe (Matthew 27:28), mocking his kingship. Even though this act degraded Jesus Christ, it also inadvertently reinforced his royal lineage (see the chronology in Matthew 1) and his fulfillment of Old Testament prophesy that the Messiah would be king (see 2 Samuel 7:12).

Biblical Footwear

Search the Scriptures

In ancient times, when you purchased something tangible, you'd usually be given a bill of sale. But if you bought a right to something, you'd be given a shoe as a token of transference. When Ruth's kinsman gave Boaz the right to Elimelech's land (and thereby the right to marry Ruth also), he "drew off his shoe" as a token of agreement. This gesture was considered solemn and binding (Ruth 4:7, 8).

When it came to footwear, children normally ran barefooted, but nearly everyone else in biblical times wore sandals. Sandals were made from leather or wooden soles that were tied to the foot by thin bands called latchets. According to custom, a person removed his or her shoes before entering a home or synagogue as a sign of respect. Tying or untying a person's shoes or washing his feet showed humility, for these tasks were reserved for the lowest household servant. (In the lands and times of the Bible, the roads were often dusty, so foot washing was part of everyday life.) Kissing a man's feet was also a way of asking for his forgiveness. For instance, when the woman described in Luke 7:45-48 kissed Jesus Christ's feet, he said to her: "Thy sins are forgiven."

Middle Eastern people sometimes greet an esteemed person, holy man, king, or elder by bowing down and touching or kissing his feet. Variations of this custom can been seen throughout the Bible. For instance, when Abigail was summoned to join David as his wife, "she arose, and bowed herself on her face to the earth, and said, 'Behold, let thine handmaid be a servant to wash the feet of the servants of my lord'" (1 Samuel 25:41). In gratitude to the prophet Elisha, the Shunnamite woman "fell at his feet, and bowed herself to the ground" (2 Kings 4:37).

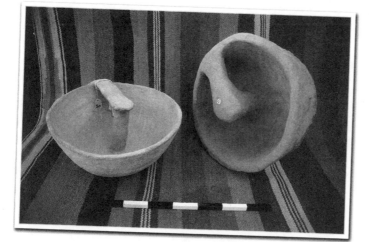

These special basins from the fourth century A.D. show the importance of foot washing in the Middle Eastern culture.

Biblical Headwear

Perhaps no other article of clothing is associated with Middle Eastern women more than the veil. Usually made from fine cloth, this thin piece of long, delicate fabric could be draped over the head and tied with twine, or wrapped around the head and neck like a scarf. Veils came in a variety of shades and were often decorated with fine embroidery. Tied together and slung over the shoulder, veils could even be used to carry things like grain, money, or sometimes babies! When Boaz gave Ruth six measures of barley, she carried it home in her veil (see Ruth 3:14, 15).

The Eastern custom of veiling the face is as old as the Bible itself, yet when a woman veiled herself varied over time. Historians say that in Old Testament days, women and girls covered their heads and faces whenever they ventured outside the home. Later, only married women veiled themselves in public. This custom is still observed in parts of the Middle East today where Muslim women are covered from head to toe in black fabric, leaving only their eyes exposed. Besides protecting her from the scorching sun, the veil also symbolized a woman's inner modesty. Note how Rebekeh veiled herself when she saw her future husband, Isaac, approaching in Genesis 24:65. To the Middle Eastern mind, modesty is essential to a woman's character and reputation. For a woman to go without a veil would be considered shameful.

While women covered their heads with veils, men wore headdresses, such as keffiyehs, skullcaps, or turbans. In parts of Arabia today, men still wear keffiyehs—a square piece of cloth tied around the head with a cord. Shepherds normally wore a skullcap or tight-fitting, brimless hat. And historians say that tur-

bans were commonplace in Old Testament times. It's possible that Abraham, Job, and Joshua wore turbans.

Experts can't seem to agree about New Testament times, though. Some say Jesus Christ definitely would have worn a turban; others say he would have worn something similar to the Arabian keffiyeh. Regardless of the style, Middle Eastern men would have worn some type of covering because of the potential danger from sun and heat stroke.

Search the Scriptures

Most men in Bible times grew beards. Men kept their beards neatly trimmed and often rubbed them with perfumed oils. (Supposedly, the perfume helped ward off lice and other vermin!) When David pretended to be insane, he drooled down his beard, for in that culture, only a crazy man would so neglect his beard (1 Samuel 21:13). If a man shaved off his beard, it meant he was in mourning (see Isaiah 15:2 and Jeremiah 48:37).

Shaving off another man's beard was considered a grave insult. When Hunan wanted to shame David's servants, he shaved off half of each of their beards (2 Samuel 10:4, 5). Additionally, it was considered an insult to touch another man's beard, unless it was done in friendship and respect (see 2 Samuel 20:9 for an example of this action done with deceit in mind).

Jewelry:
A Pearl of Great Price

In many ancient Near Eastern cultures, women typically wore lots of jewelry: nose rings, bracelets, and long, braided necklaces. They also liked to adorn long hair with gold, pearls, or beads. Jewelry is more than decoration to Middle Eastern women, who view jewelry as tokens of their family's love. The more gold a woman has, Middle Eastern women might say, the more she is loved. Rich women might wear gold, silver, and precious stones like emeralds and rubies. Poor peasant women would wear some sort of bauble—brass earrings or bone bracelets. On their wedding day, Near Eastern brides, and sometimes bridegrooms, wore plenty of jewelry in honor of their special occasion (see Isaiah 61:10).

Men usually did not wear much jewelry—perhaps a hoop in the ear or a ring on the finger. The head of a family might wear a signet ring, a band that showed the family's

seal and represented his familial authority (see Genesis 38:18). Signets were often used as signatures. For example, a man would stamp his signet ring into the melted wax on a sealed document. The stamp of a king was final (see Esther 8:8 and Daniel 6:17). Men might also wear gold chains around the neck or face. In the ancient Near East, rows of gold chains symbolized love and honor. When Pharaoh elevated Joseph, he put a gold chain around his neck (Genesis 41:42). Gold chains draped around a wife's neck by her husband indicated his love and respect for her (Song of Solomon 1:10).

In the lands and times of the Bible, clothing not only protected a man from the elements, it was an expression of his place in society, his state of mind, or even his relationship to God. By his garments alone you could tell if a person were wealthy or poor, shepherd or scribe, freeborn or slave.

Search the Scriptures

Clothed

Genesis 3:21
Leviticus 8:7
2 Chronicles 6:41
Esther 4:2
Psalm 93:1
Psalm 104:1
Proverbs 31:21
Matthew 25:36
Mark 1:6
Mark 15:17
1 Peter 5:5

Clothes

Genesis 49:11
Exodus 12:34
Matthew 24:18
Luke 19:36
Acts 7:58
Acts 22:23

Washing Clothes

Exodus 19:10, 14
Leviticus 11:25, 40
Numbers 8:7
Numbers 19:7
Numbers 31:24
2 Samuel 19:24

Covered Head

2 Samuel 15:30
Esther 6:12
Psalm 140:7
Jeremiah 14:3, 4
1 Corinthians 11:4

Robe/Robes

Leviticus 8:7
1 Samuel 18:4
1 Samuel 24:4, 11
1 Chronicles 15:27
Jonah 3:6
Matthew 27:28, 31
Luke 15:22
Luke 23:11
Luke 20:46
Revelation 6:11
Revelation 7:9, 13, 14

Sandals

Mark 6:9
Acts 12:8

Shoes

Exodus 3:5
Deuteronomy 25:9, 10
Ruth 4:7
Ezekiel 24:17
Amos 2:6
Amos 8:6
Luke 15:22

Under Tunic

Materials Needed:

- 1 pillow case (ask Mom first —she won't want it back!)
- scissors
- yard stick and pencil or chalk (to mark cloth)

Directions:

1. Take pillow case and cut along the lines as shown in the drawing.
2. Slip head and arms through holes.

Please note that boys garments should come to their knees, and girls garments should come to their ankles.

Middle Eastern Wardrobe

(Note to teacher/parent: The following patterns require no sewing and are very simple so that children can make the clothing themselves. However, if a more sophisticated design involving sewing is desired, check patterns in fabric stores. There are several that will yield some authentic-looking garments (for example, see McCall's pattern numbers 8435 and 9436 and Simplicity's pattern numbers 8152 and 8153).

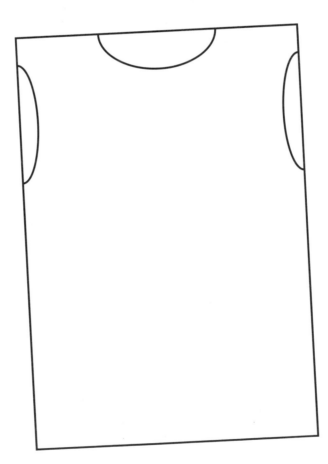

Outer Tunic

Materials Needed:

- 2 to 3 yards of fabric (lightweight)
- scissors
- yard stick and pencil or chalk (to mark cloth)

Directions:

1. Fold fabric as shown.
2. Cut along the folded edge.
3. Adjust the length for individual boys and girls. Arms on tunic should be mid-length. (A full-length sleeve would require sewing.)
4. Slip over head. (The under tunic should be covered.)

Please note that boys' garments should come to their knees, and girls' garments should come to their ankles.

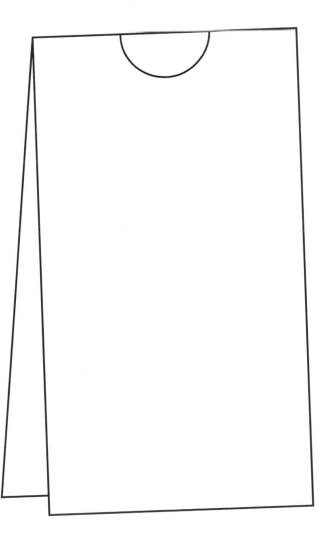

Coat/Robe

Materials Needed:

- 2 to 3 yards of fabric (medium to heavy weight)
- scissors
- yard stick and pencil or chalk (to mark cloth)

Directions:

1. Make the robe exactly as you made the outer tunic.
2. Cut the neck opening with the cloth folded in half, then cut the front panel down the middle to open the robe. The back will stay in one piece, but the garment will not stay on without a belt.

Please note that boys' garments should come to their knees, and girls' garments should come to their ankles.

Boys can wear a heavy piece of fabric over shoulders for a mantle. They also can try "girding up their loins"—remove coat, then pull up other garments between legs and tuck into belt.

Girls can decorate the neckline of their garments (except under tunic) with fabric paint or embroidery. Women in the Middle East commonly decorated these necklines. Sometimes the patterns showed where the woman was from and from what family. Girls can also wear any jewelry they can find—ankle bracelets, earrings, bangles, etc. (Remember, there were no digital watches in Bible times!)

Linen Belt or Girdle

Materials Needed:
- 2 to 3 yards of medium to heavy linen
- scissors
- yard stick and pencil or chalk (to mark cloth)

Directions:
1. Cut a piece of linen 6 inches wide and long enough to go around a child's waist several times.
2. Wrap the belt around the waist and tie it in front. Experiment making folds in the belt to use like "pockets." (See if you can carry something without dropping it.)

Simple Purse

Materials Needed:
- 4-by-12-inch piece of cloth
- 12-inch-long piece of cord
- needle and thread

Directions:
1. Fold over 1/2 inch of one end of the cloth and stitch it so you can run the cord through it. Do the same to the other end. Make sure you fold both sides toward the inside of the bag.
2. Fold the cloth in half so that the two stitched ends meet with the folded portions on the outside.
3. Stitch up both sides of the bag leaving the holes open for the cord.
4. Turn the bag inside out (so that all the folds and stitches are inside the bag).
5. Run the cord through both holes and tie the ends together. To close the purse, simply pull the cord tight.

Keffiyeh or Headdress
for Boys

Materials Needed:

- 1 bandanna
- 2 yards of medium to heavy linen
- scissors
- yard stick and pencil or chalk (to mark cloth)

Directions:

1. Cut the cloth to 20 inches by 40 inches.
2. Place lengthwise over head and wrap a twisted bandanna around head to hold cloth in place. Keffiyeh should cover head and shoulders.

Veil or Headdress
for Girls

Materials Needed:

- 1 bandanna
- 1 large fashion scarf (found in department stores)

Directions:

1. Wear scarf over head and around shoulders. Try covering your face like the ancients did.
2. Twist the bandanna until it's a thin cord, then place the bandanna over the veil to keep the veil in place.

How to Wrap a Turban

Materials Needed:

- a piece of cloth about 12 inches wide and 5 feet long. Thin cloth, such as gauze or a lightweight broadcloth, will work best. Be patient; this isn't as easy as it looks!

Step 1 Tuck the short end under your chin (or hold it in your mouth).

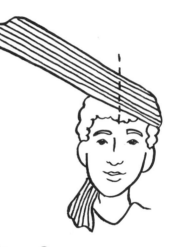

Step 2 Wrap the long end upwards around your head and across your forehead.

Step 3 Hold the cloth at the center of your forehead and give it one full twist downward.

Step 4 Continue wrapping the cloth downward and around the back of your head toward the front.

Step 6 Tuck the remaining short bit of cloth into the wrapped cloth snugly. The back of your head will still be exposed, and you will still have the short end tucked under your chin or in your mouth.

Step 5 Wrap the long end upwards around your forehead and give it a full twist, as in step 3. Repeat steps 3 through 5 until you have only a short bit of cloth left to wrap.

Step 7 Find the first layer (against your scalp) and gently slide it out from under the outer layers until it covers the back of your head and tuck it under the other side of the turban. Finally tuck the short end that was under your chin into the back of the wrappings.

Paper Bag Robe

Materials Needed:
- a large paper grocery bag for each child
- scissors
- paint, markers, or crayons

Directions:
1. In the center of the bottom of the bag, cut out a hole large enough for the child's head.
2. In the bottom of both sides of the bag, cut out a hole for the child's arm.
3. Cut the center of one face of the bag from top to bottom into the hole for the child's head. You should now have an article that resembles a coat or robe. You can have the children decorate their robes with paint, markers, or crayons.

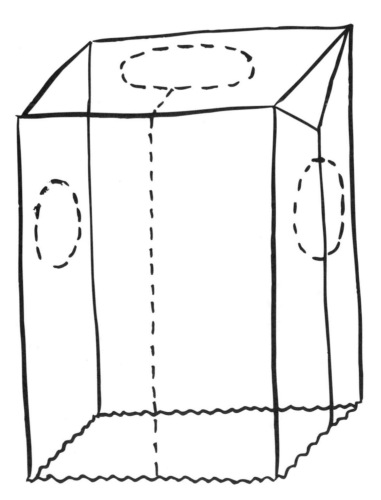

Sandals

Materials Needed:

- a 1-foot-square piece of corrogated cardboard for each child
- two 18-inch-long pieces of heavy string for each child
- scissors or utility knife
- an awl or hole punch

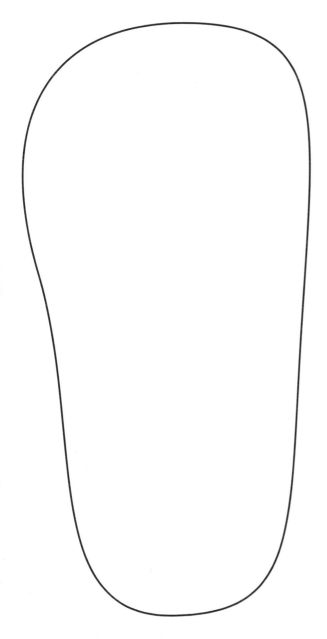

Directions:

1. Using either the pattern provided or each chld's own shoes, trace a slightly oversized outline of a pair of feet (right and left feet are necessary) on the piece of cardboard.

2. Using either the scissors or the utility knife, cut out the soles of your sandals. (Corrogated cardboard is difficult to cut, even for adults. You might want to do this step before class or have enough help to get thorugh this step quickly and safely.)

3. Punch two holes in the cardboard on both sides of the ball of each child's feet. You might also want to punch one hole on each side of each child's heel.

4. Lace the string through the holes so that they cross over top of the child's foot. You can tie the string off here or wrap some of the excess around the child's ankles. If you have holes near the heels, lace the string through these holes and tie around the ankles.

Chapter Four

The Role of the Scroll

"Forasmuch as ye are manifestly declared to be the epistle of Christ ministered by us, written not with ink, but with the Spirit of the living God; not in tables of stone, but in fleshly tables of the heart" (2 Corinthians 3:3).

The double blast of the trumpet signaled the start of the Sabbath. Jesus slowly made his way to the synagogue along with the other men of Nazareth. Entering the porch, he removed his sandals, covered his head with his mantle and quietly went in. The white limestone floor felt cool beneath his bare feet as he walked towards the back of the room and sat down. Other men of the working class sat nearby: Josiah, the tent-maker, Michiah the mason. Familiar faces. Old Nahor the blacksmith sat cross-legged near the north column, just as he had done since Jesus was a boy.

The synagogue leaders filed in and sat down on the benches at the front of the room. When the room had settled, one of the elders stood up to pray:

"Blessed be thou, O Lord, King of the world, who formest the light and createst the darkness, who makest peace, and createst everything; who in mercy, givest light to the earth."

After the prayer, the men sang psalms in deep, rich tones that reverberated throughout the room. The synagogue ruler stood up to read the first lesson, from the Book of the Law. All listened in quiet contemplation as he read the familiar words from Deuteronomy. Then, Jesus stood up to read.

All eyes fastened upon Jesus as he made his way to the lectern at the center of the synagogue. He gestured for the scroll. The chazan, the synagogue servant, scrambled to his feet and handed Jesus the book of the prophet Isaiah. Jesus placed the leather scroll on the stone lectern and carefully unrolled it several feet. He scanned the full ten-inch width, looking for the place. Satisfied that he'd found the passage, Jesus paused to look around the room. Then, in a voice that flooded the synagogue, Jesus read:

"The spirit of the Lord is upon me, for he hath anointed me to heal the

brokenhearted, to preach deliverance to the captives, and recovering of sight to the blind, to set at liberty them that are bruised, to preach the acceptable year of the Lord."

The previous scene describes Jesus Christ reading from the book of Isaiah in his hometown synagogue (Luke 4:16-19). But what did the book of Isaiah look like, or other books used in Bible times? Archaeological discoveries and historical records show that books in antiquity were rolled up pieces of material called scrolls, which were unrolled as they were read. Scrolls were ordinarily made out of cloth, leather, or papyrus, although some clay, stone, and wooden tablets have also been discovered. Ancient people even had a type of scrap paper. In cities throughout the Bible lands, archaeologists have discovered thousands of ostraca, pieces of clay jars, inscribed with statistics, calculations, and even grocery lists.

Papyrus Scrolls

Experts say that throughout antiquity most scrolls were made out of papyrus, a tall water plant that grows along the Nile River and in parts of Palestine. Egyptians invented the method of writing on papyrus (where we get our English word "paper"). To make paper from this lanky plant, Egyptians first sliced strips from the stem's pith, then laid them out on a board. A second layer was crisscrossed on top. After drying in the sun, the pages were smoothed out with a stone. Papyrus scrolls were durable, lightweight, and easy to store. Mistakes could be easily washed away with water or rubbed out with the blunt side of a pen. Egyptians also used papyrus (sometimes called "bulrushes") to make baskets, ropes, sandals, and clothing. The baby Moses was put into a papyrus basket made waterproof by tar-like pitch (Exodus 2:3).

Historians say that by New Testament times, scrolls were commonly made from leather, usually sheep or goat hides. To make a leather scroll, hides were cleaned, stretched on a frame, then dried in the sun. Writing was done on the hair side of the skin, so this was scraped smooth with a stone or shell. Several pieces of leather would be sewn together to made one scroll. (Some estimate that Paul's Epistle to the Romans, for instance, would have required a scroll about thirteen feet long!) Leather scrolls were usually stored in clay jars so that the hides would not dry out and subsequently crack or break.

Search the Scriptures

In the ancient Near East, sons were sometimes looked after by a schoolmaster—a trusty slave who watched over a six-year-old boy until puberty. The schoolmaster would escort the child to and from school and guard him from physical or moral evil. The Bible declares that the Law was our schoolmaster, until the greater came: Christ and justification by faith (see Galatians 3:24).

According to ancient custom, teachers stood up whenever they read the Scriptures but sat down to give their exposition (see John 8:2 and Matthew 5:1). In a school setting, a teacher would sit on a bench, a rock, or something similar while pupils literally sat at his feet.

In the ancient Near East, disciples were often called sons, and teachers were called fathers. When the Bible mentions "sons of the prophets," it's likely referring to students who studied under master teachers, not boys whose fathers were prophets (see 1 Kings 20:35; 2 Kings 2:3-15; 2 Kings 4:38; 2 Kings 6:1).

Pen and Ink

To write on papyrus or leather scrolls, people used an assortment of pens and inks. Archaeologists have unearthed a fascinating array of ornate pens fashioned out of ivory, silver, or gold, some studded with precious stones. But the instrument most commonly used for writing was the simple reed pen, made from a type of water grass. The reed was sliced at one end to form a tiny brush; the writer then painted his letters on the scroll. Or, the reed could be cut at an angle and used like a quill feather pen. Special chisels were used to inscribe letters on stone tablets. A metal pen, or stylus, was used to write on wooden or clay tablets and might be diamond-tipped for durability. The prophet Jeremiah said Judah's sin was written "with a pen of iron, and with the point of a diamond; it is graven upon the table of their heart," indicating both the depth and permanence of their transgressions (Jeremiah 17:1).

Most ancient writings were done in black ink, made from a mixture of ash, water, and tree gum or oil, although red and yellow pigments were also used. Scientists marvel at the permanence of this ink, for some still-legible writings date back to 3000 B.C.! Ink was usually dried into cakes (the writer then had to wet his pen before writing), or liquid ink was carried in an inkhorn, usually a hollowed-out ram's horn. Scribes were easily identified because these inkhorns typically hung from their belts.

After the synagogue service, doctors of the law would sometimes meet in the temple to discuss the Scriptures. When the boy Jesus met with the doctors in Jerusalem, "sitting in the midst of the doctors, both hearing them and asking them questions," he was following this custom. Those who heard Jesus were astonished because of his understanding, not simply because he was talking with the doctors (Luke 2:46, 47).

To erase mistakes on a scroll, the writer could rub off the ink with the blunt side of the pen, scrape it off with a knife, or wash it away with water. Or he could blot out the wet ink with a rag. In Psalm 51, David might be referring to this thorough type of erasure when he asks God to blot out his transgression, wash his iniquity, and cleanse his sin (Psalms 51:1, 2).

In Bible times, Jewish men sometimes wore phylacteries, small leather boxes containing Scriptures, on their arms or foreheads. The intent was to continually remind themselves of the Scriptures (a literal application of Exodus 13:9, 16; Deuteronomy 6:8; 11:18). However, when Jesus Christ said the Pharisees made "broad their phylacteries" (Matthew 23:5), he was reproving their hypocrisy. Ordinarily, phylacteries were tiny boxes, not prominent ones intended for show. "But all their works they do for to be seen of men" (Matthew 23:5).

Scribes

In the lands and times of the Bible, most of the writing was left to scribes—men especially trained in reading and writing. Scribes were hired to draft letters, draw up marriage or divorce contracts, write bills of sale, take records from dictation, and the like. Kings employed their own scribes (2 Kings 12:10). The scribe's role in Israel's history, however, changed over time.

Initially, the Jewish scribes or sopherim meticulously copied the Scriptures. So careful were the sopherim that they would count each letter in their work to be sure nothing was omitted or added. Historians say that by the time of David and Solomon's reign, scribes had become public officials. After the Babylonian captivity, scribes returned to copying holy writings or recorded matters relating exclusively to the Temple. But by Jesus Christ's day, scribes had re-established themselves as influential interpreters of the Scriptures.

In Memphis, Egypt, the photographer's friend "Sammi" shows the progression from papyrus plant to paper.

Education in Old Testament Times

That's not to say that scribes were the only literate people in ancient times, for in some parts of the ancient Near East, children attended school and subsequently learned to read and to write. For instance, archaeologists know that schools existed in the city of Ur where Abraham grew up. Called "tablet houses" for the type of soft clay tablets used in the classroom, these schools typically trained students in religion, government, and commerce. Excavations of this city reveal that students learned subjects, such as writing, dictation, grammar, and arithmetic.

By the time of Moses, education had become quite sophisticated in some parts of the ancient world. Egyptian schools were reputed to be among the finest in the world. In addition to language, Egyptian students learned astronomy, architecture, trigonometry, as well as advanced sciences like medicine, anatomy, chemistry, and metallurgy. Some historians believe that Moses, because he was the adopted son of an Egyptian princess, would likely have attended a prestigious school called "The Temple of the Sun in Heliopolis."

Attending a school like the Temple of the Sun certainly wasn't the norm in Old Testament times, for many people simply educated their children at home. Mothers taught their daughters domestic skills, although some girls might go on to study midwifery or music under another woman's tutelage. When boys were old enough, their fathers usually taught them the family trade. So important was this apprenticeship that Middle Easterners have a saying: "He who does not teach his son a useful trade is bringing up a thief." For Israel, education was primarily the parent's responsibility. According to the Law, parents were to diligently teach their children to love God and to obey his commandments, as is explained in Deuteronomy 6:4-7: "Hear, O Israel: The Lord our God is one Lord: And thou shalt love the Lord thy God with all thine heart, and with all thy soul, and with all thy might. And these words, which I command thee this day, shall be in thine heart: and thou shalt teach them diligently unto thy children, and shalt talk of them when thou sittest in thine house, and when thou walkest by the way, and when thou liest down, and when thou risest up."

In addition, select Israelite students could attend a special "school" called the "sons of the prophets" or "company of prophets" (1 Samuel 19:20). Under the tutelage of a spiritual elder, young men were trained as future prophets who would teach the Law of God to the people. In addition to the Scriptures, pupils studied Israel's history, sacred music, and poetry. It's believed that schools of the prophets were located at Bethel, Rama, Jericho (2 Kings 2:5), and Gilgal (2 Kings 4:38).

Education in New Testament Times

Synagogue at Capernaum

By New Testament times, formal schooling was commonplace in many cities. Historians say that in the apostle Paul's day, for example, there were twenty grammar schools in Rome for both boys and girls. Jewish boys would have attended synagogue schools, for their education system was based in the Aramaic and Hebrew languages, not in Latin or Greek. Some historians believe that the Greek and Roman culture had little influence on Jewish education because of this language barrier. Yet in several instances, records show that Jewish children did sometimes enroll in city schools, called gymnasiums, even though the price for admission meant worshiping the gods of the city.

Gymnasium Schools

Centered on athletics, gymnasium schools trained young boys, ages seven to twenty, in sports, such as running, jumping, throwing the discus and the javelin, wrestling, and boxing. Students also were given instruction in music, art, and literature. Unlike synagogue schools where the Scriptures were emphasized, gymnasiums encouraged physical achievement and competition. (Gymnasium comes from the Greek word *gymnos*, meaning nude, for boys trained in the nude.) Some cities had separate gymnasium schools for girls.

While Roman and Greek schools admitted girls, Jewish synagogue schools allowed only boys. In New Testament times, Jewish girls were educated at home by their mothers. Nearly everything a mother taught her daughter revolved around observing the Law, from food preparation to making clothes to observing the Sabbath. What boys learned doctrinally at school, girls learned practically at home. Girls could also learn the Scriptures at the weekly synagogue service. Sitting apart in the women's gallery, they listened as elders prayed, read, and expounded the Scriptures.

Synagogue at Gamla

Synagogue Schools

For Jewish boys in New Testament times, the foundation of education was the Torah—the first five books of the Bible. Beginning at five years old, boys would spend six half days a week at an elementary synagogue school called *bet hasefer*, or house of the book. Once he could write and read the Hebrew alphabet, the boy was taught the Torah—his only reading material. Students learned mostly by rote memorization; long passages of the Torah were recited daily at the *bet hasefer*.

From ten years old onward, boys attended a *bet talmud*, or the house of learning. In addition to the Torah, they studied the oral law, later written down as the Mishnah, as well as mathematics, music, art, and philosophy. Some offered physical training, too. Memorization, oral recitation, and argumentative reasoning based in Scripture were key teaching methods used in these synagogue schools. Many say that while growing up Nazareth, Jesus might have attended the synagogue school there.

For advanced students, or for those wishing to become scribes or doctors of the law, there was the *bet midrash*, or house of study where pupils learned from several master teachers. In addition to memorization of Scripture, pupils learned writing, recitation, astronomy, natural science, and geography, but only as it related to the Scriptures. When a student could correctly answer a difficult matter of the law, he was considered an advanced scholar, or rabbi. Some rabbis would go on to devote themselves exclusively to teaching. Small groups of disciples would follow the rabbi—eating, working, and living with him. Teaching by parable was a popular teaching tool used by rabbis.

In synagogue schools, supplies were nominal. For notebooks, students might use wooden boards covered with wax and a pointed stick for a pen. When the board was full, another layer of warmed wax was spread on top. Sometimes a student carried a tiny scroll with him to memorize a few verses at home. Synagogue schools typically had few books, and fewer had their own copies of the Scriptures. (Most had only smaller portions.) Because Jesus Christ was so knowledgeable of the Scriptures as a child, some believe that the Nazareth synagogue school probably had

Synagogue at Masada

its own copy of the Scriptures. Consider this passage from Luke: "And it came to pass, that after three days they found him in the temple, sitting in the midst of the doctors, both hearing them, and asking them questions. And all that heard him were astonished at his understanding and answers" (Luke 2:46, 47).

Books were scarce in Bible times, and public libraries as we know them were virtually non-existent. Yet archaeologists have unearthed the remains of several ancient libraries, such as the famed Alexandrian library in Egypt. This mammoth building once housed more than half a million volumes, mostly papyrus scrolls. Despite being damaged in several wars, the Alexandrian library remained open until A.D. 4.

In 1947, a shepherd boy discovered ruins from another ancient library in caves near the Dead Sea. While tending his flocks, he stumbled upon thousands of scrolls and scroll fragments. These are the famous Dead Sea Scrolls, the largest body of scrolls ever found to date. Among the discoveries was a copy of the entire book of Isaiah—the only one like it in the world. This eight-inch-wide, twenty-foot-long leather scroll dates back to 100 B.C.

"And he closed the book, and he gave it again to the minister, and sat down. And the eyes of all them that were in the synagogue were fastened on him. And he began to say unto them, This day is this Scripture fulfilled in your ears" (Luke 4:20, 21).

Phylacteries

In Bible times Jewish men wore phylacteries, small leather boxes containing passages of Scriptures, on their left arms or on their foreheads. The arm phylactery was attached by winding a long strap from the box, down the arm, and around the hand and fingers. It was thus placed so that whenever the box touched the body, the Scriptures would be near the heart. Head phylacteries were similarly fastened by a long strap wound around the head so that the Scriptures remained at the forefront of the mind. Some sources say that the Pharisees in Jesus' time wore the phylacteries in the palm of the left hand instead of on the arm.

Materials:

- 1 tiny box (about the size of a small matchbox)
- paper and pen
- a hot glue gun and glue sticks
- new shoe laces or 1 to 2 feet of ribbon (extra long for the arm phylactery)

Directions:

1. Copy down your favorite verse of Scripture on a piece of paper. (Some sources say that four passages from the Law of Moses were written in Hebrew and carried in the phylacteries: Exodus 13:1-10; Exodus 11-16; Deuteronomy 6:4-9; and Deuteronomy 11:13-21.)
2. Tuck the paper in the box, and close the lid tightly. (Tape it closed if necessary.)
3. With hot glue, attach the ribbon or shoelace to the center of the bottom of the box.
4. Attach the arm phylactery by winding the ribbon around the arm, hand, and fingers. The box should be firmly in place. (Note: it's not easy, so keep trying!)
5. Attach the head phylactery by winding the ribbon around the head, placing the box in the middle of your forehead.
6. Try wearing the phylacteries for a day to see how often it reminds you of God's Word.

Greek Alphabet

Greek was the language of trade and commerce of the whole Mediterranean world in Jesus' time. Even the Jews and Romans spoke and wrote this language in order to communicate effectively with people from other cultures. In fact, because Greek was so common, it helped the new church spread the Gospel more quickly to all parts of the world!

Notice that the letters are very similar to many letters in English. Using the key provided, try to write a message about Jesus' love for all people of all nations. You may have to spell words phonetically (breaking words into sounds rather than exact letters).

α	β	γ	δ	∈	ζ
short a	b	g	d	e	z

η	θ	ι	κ	λ	μ
long a	th	i	k	l	m

ν	ξ	ο	π	ρ	σ
n	x	short o	p	r	s

τ	υ	φ	χ	ψ	ω
t	u	f, ph	c, ch	ps	long o

Writing on Wax Tablets

Materials Needed:

- Candles or paraffin (often available at craft or hardware stores)
- a pointed stick (or wooden cuticle stick)
- lid of shoe box (or similar size)
- aluminum foil
- wax paper
- tape

Directions:

1. Line the shoe box lid with wax paper, then aluminum foil
2. Tape the edges so that it stays in place.
3. Melt the candles or paraffin using a double boiler (paraffin usually has directions for melting on the label).
4. Pour a thin layer of melted wax into the shoe box lid.
5. Let the wax cool until surface is firm, but not too hard. (If it's sticky to the touch, let it cool longer.)
6. Using the pointed stick, practice writing a verse.

Clay Tablet and Stylus

Materials:

- modeling clay (DAS terra-cotta clay is recommended)
- pointed stick or wooden cuticle stick

Directions:

1. Shape clay into a 6-inch-by-8-inch rectangular tablet.
2. Make surface smooth
3. With a stylus, practice writing different letters.
4. Allow to dry for about 24 hours.

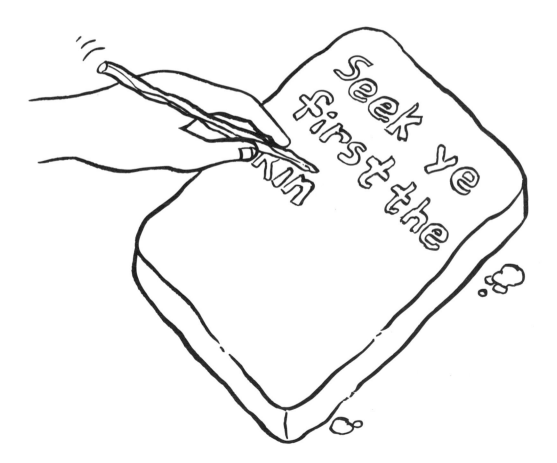

Cloth and Leather Scrolls

Materials Needed:

- 9-inch-wide by 2-foot-long piece of leather, fake leather, or a stiff fabric (canvas or denim)
- two 1-inch-thick by 9-inch-long dowels
- stapler or glue
- pen and ink (calligraphy style if possible) or a permanent marker

Directions:

1. Spread out the scroll material and write a message or Scripture verse on it. Be sure to leave enough space at each end to attach the dowels.
2. Attach the scroll material to the dowels with the stapler or with glue. Let your ink and glue dry before rolling up the scroll.

86

Sealing a Document With a Signet Ring

Materials Needed:

- a candle
- a ring with a raised image on it (you can use costume jewelry, get a plastic ring from a party supply store, or use rubber stamps with raised images)
- paper (preferably parchment paper, available at stationery stores)

Note: some stationery stores also have sealing wax kits.

Directions:

1. Fold a letter so that the last flap ends up in the middle of the letter.
2. Light a candle and drip a small amount of wax (about the size of a quarter) in the middle of the letter over the edge of the last flap.
3. As the wax begins to cool and solidify, impress the ring or stamp in the wax.
4. Let the wax cool completely. The document is sealed once wax is thoroughly cooled.

Try sealing a rolled letter. This is how most letters looked in Bible times.

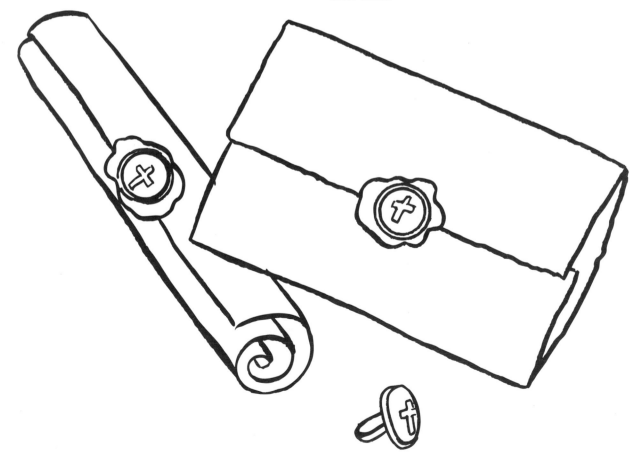

Twenty Questions Game

In ancient days, schools were much different from what they are now. Most teachers simply traveled from place to place doing their everyday things, but their students followed along, asking questions every step of the way. The Socratic Method, named for the Greek philosopher Socrates who lived in the fifth century before Christ, was a common method of questioning others in order to help them express what they were thinking and learning more clearly, with the expectation of learning the truth.

The modern game "Twenty Questions" is very similar to the Socratic Method. Help your students learn facts about their lessons by thinking of a person, place, or thing in the story and allowing your students to ask twenty questions to try to determine what you are thinking about.

Here's a list of biblical words that you can have your class guess after asking twenty questions:

People
Adam
Eve
Abraham
Joseph
David
Jonah
Jesus
Peter
Paul

Places
Garden of Eden
Egypt
Canaan
Jerusalem
Rome

Things
Altar
Ark
Ark of the Covenant
Ten Commandments
Sling
Lamp

Animals
Camel
Donkey
Lamb
Big Fish
Bull
Dove
Raven

Plants
Olive Tree
Sycamore Tree
Hyssop
Wheat
Tares

Make Your Classroom Look Like a Synagogue

Using the sample floor plan, rearrange the furniture in your classroom to create a synagogue. You should have an ark—a place to store the scroll of the Law (A); a bema—a raised platform from which to read the scroll (B); a luach—a desk or lectern from which the scrolls are read (C); a genizah—a place to store scrolls that are not currently in use (D); and a few rows of benches (E).

Have your students imagine what it would have been like to worship in a first century synagogue, or perhaps attend school in the synagogue.

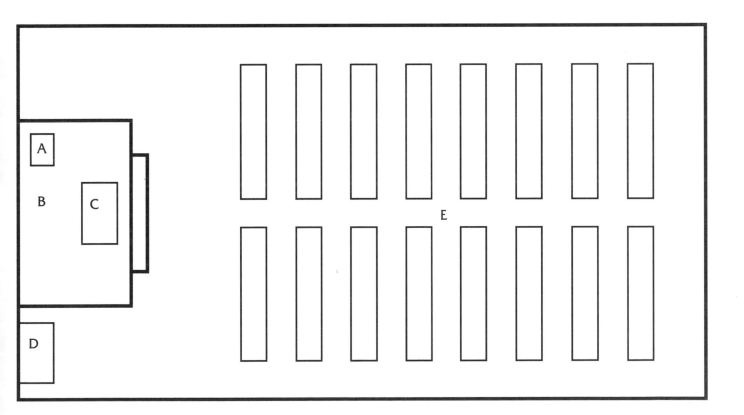

Classroom Exercises
for Students

1. Have students copy passages of the Bible, keeping a running count of number of letters used per line. Compare for accuracy. This will give them some indication of the painstaking care scribes used in copying the Scriptures.

2. Have a competition to see who can memorize the longest passage of Scripture. Pair people off, or hold the competition according to age groups.

3. Write a long verse of Scripture on several index cards, breaking up the verse into phrases. Then, mix up the cards and have students work together to reassemble the verse correctly. You can do this with a long passage from the Bible, one verse, or all the books of the Bible. See who can reassemble the cards the quickest.

4. Practice memorizing the order of the books of the Bible in your classroom using rote memorization. Explain that this is one way in which students learned in synagogue schools.

5. For older children, ask complex questions that require reasoning based on their knowledge of the Scriptures. You can put forth an erroneous premise, and ask the students why it is wrong and how to correct it based on biblical reasoning.

6. Organize a work project with the older children while teaching a principle from the Bible. Reinforce the lesson throughout the day, as you work, eat lunch, or take breaks. At midday, take the time to expound the Scriptures, encouraging questions and answers. (You assume the role of the teacher while your students play the role of disciples. Therefore, you will sit on a chair, step, or the like while they sit at your feet.) This will, to some degree, illustrate to them how ancient teachers and their disciples worked, ate, and lived together.

7. Set up an informal, congenial debate between two older children or two teams, the intent being to sharpen reasoning and communication skills. Topics for debate can include: creation vs. evolution; truth vs. tradition; biblical Christianity vs. humanism.

8. Discuss popular trends and why they may or may not be supported by Scripture. Have students supply verses and/or sound biblical reasoning to support their views.

Search the Scriptures

Here is a list of Scriptures that mention various aspects of learning, writing, and God's Word.

Scroll/Book

Exodus 24:7
2 Kings 22:8-10
2 Kings 23:13
2 Chronicles 17:9
2 Chronicles 34:14-31
Ezra 4:15
Nehemiah 8:1-18
Esther 6:1
Job 19:23, 24
Isaiah 29:11,12
Isaiah 34:4
Jeremiah 36:1-32
Jeremiah 45:1
Ezekiel 2:9,10
2 Timothy 4:13
Revelation 1:11
Revelation 3:5
Revelation 5:1-9
Revelation 6:14
Revelation 20:12-15
Revelation 22:19

Scribes

2 Samuel 8:17
2 Samuel 20:25
2 Kings 12:10
2 Kings 18:18
2 Kings 22:8-10
2 Kings 25:19
1 Chronicles 24:6
1 Chronicles 27:32
Ezra 7:6-21
Nehemiah 8:1-28
Jeremiah 8:8
Jeremiah 36:1-32
Jeremiah 52:25
Matthew 2:4
Matthew 7:29
Matthew 8:19
Matthew 12:38
Matthew 16:21
Matthew 20:18
Matthew 27:41
Mark 9:11-16
Mark 12:28-38
Luke 5:21-30
Luke 20:1-46
Acts 4:5
Acts 6:12
Acts 23:9
1 Corinthians 1:20

Blotting Out

Exodus 32:32,33
Numbers 5:23
Deuteronomy 25:19
Deuteronomy 29:20
Psalms 51:1,2
Psalms 69:28
Acts 3:19
Colossians 2:14
Revelation 3:5

Pen

Judges 5:14
Job 19:24
Psalms 45:1
Isaiah 8:1
Jeremiah 8:8
Jeremiah 17:1
3 John 13

Chapter Five

Family Life

"For this cause, I bow my knees unto the Father or our Lord Jesus Christ, Of whom the whole family in heaven and earth is named" (Ephesians 3:14, 15).

It was a warm summer night in the village of Beer-sheba. Samuel decided that he and his grandsons had better sleep on the rooftop tonight, rather than in the sweltering house below. So he tucked a mat under his arm and called the boys to follow him. Together, they climbed the stairs to their lofty bed.

"Tells us about the stars again, grandfather," Caleb said once they were on the roof.

"And all their names, too," Joshua added.

Samuel unrolled the mat and sat down on it. Immediately, his grandsons climbed onto their grandfather's lap, Caleb on his right knee and Joshua on his left. Samuel put his arms around the boys. Five year-old Joshua leaned back, his head resting against the old man's long, white-gray beard. Caleb stared up into the starry sky.

"God knows the number of stars, Caleb, and God

knows all their names, Joshua," the old man answered. A soft breeze brushed over them carrying with it a hint of freshly cut hay. From their position on the rooftop, the three could hear cattle lowing in the distance and soft voices talking in the house below. The stars glistened above them in the great black expanse.

"In the beginning, God created the heavens and the earth," Samuel continued. "And he made two great lights—do you remember what they are called to do?"

"The greater to rule the day and the lesser to rule the night," seven year-old Caleb proudly answered.

"Very good, my son. You listened well," Samuel said. "And why did God create the stars, Joshua?"

"For signs and for seasons, grandfather," the little boy answered.

"Yes, my son. You also listened well," Samuel said. Joshua nestled into the crook of his grandfather's arm and closed his eyes. Soon, the sound of Samuel's gentle, even voice lulled the little boy to sleep.

"The heavens declare the glory of God and the sky shows forth his handiwork," Samuel said. "Do you know what that constellation is?" Samuel pointed to a cluster of stars.

"Leo, " Caleb promptly answered.

"And what does it represent?" Samuel asked.

"He's the lion of the tribe of Judah, grandfather. The Messiah will come out Judah," Caleb answered.

"Yes, and what is the brightest star called in Leo? Do you remember what I taught you last night?"

"Regul, Regul…" Caleb stammered.

"Regulus. The king star," Samuel said. "And what about that constellation there, just above Leo?"

"That's easy—Virgo!"

"Good. Now, which is the brightest constellation of all? Can you find it?"

Caleb searched the sky. "There! I see it. There's Orion," Caleb exclaimed.

"And what are the three bright stars in Orion called?" Samuel prodded.

"The Band of Orion, grandfather," Caleb said yawning. He stretched his arms up over his head then slumped against his grandfather's chest.

"Yes, and tonight I will teach you about Orion, Caleb. Can you see that big, bright star in Orion's right shoulder?"

"Yes, grandfather, I see it," Caleb whispered, his eyes heavy with sleep.

"It is called Betelgeuse—one of the brightest stars in Orion. It means the coming of the Righteous Branch, the Messiah," Samuel said. "The Messiah—Shiloh—will come, Caleb, and he will bring peace."

"Messiah will come…." Caleb echoed and then drifted off to sleep.

Samuel laid the boys down on the mat and then sat cross-legged nearby. He gazed up into the sky for a long, long time.

"Until Shiloh comes…." Samuel said.

Family life in the ancient Near East varied within cultures, yet some elements remain constant. For instance, in much of the ancient Near East, societies were patriarchal, or father-ruled. Roles within the family remained clear-cut. Fathers ruled over their families, protecting and providing for them, while mothers governed the household. Children worked closely with their parents, either at home with mother or with father at his trade. The family often included grandparents, aunts, uncles, and cousins, who might all live together under one roof, or in an adjoining house, or at least in the same village or city. To the Middle Eastern mind, families were God-appointed; the unity within the family was therefore all-important. Tribal fidelity, that is, loyalty to extended family, often transcended national loyalty.

Family Life

Father's Role

In ancient times, the term "father" referred to any man who headed up a tribe, a community, a city, or a family. An esteemed elder in a village, for instance, might be called "father" of that village. Father could also mean originator, like Jubal, "the father of all such as handle the harp and organ" (Genesis 4:21). Within the family, father ruled with authority; his decisions typically went unchallenged. In addition, he oversaw most of the heavy labor like building houses, digging wells, and taking care of flocks or fields. If he were a craftsman, such as a carpenter or potter, he was sure to pass on those skills to his sons, becaue Middle Easterners believe the saying: "He who doesn't teach his son a useful trade is bringing up a thief." Reputable fathers were often chosen as village elders.

Mother's Role

A woman's role in ancient times varied with the culture. Some ancient societies were matriarchal, or mother-ruled. Some elevated women in society, affording them similar rank to men. Egypt, for instance, was ruled by queens as well as by kings. But through the years, many Middle Eastern cultures degraded women, treating them as little more than slaves. Among poor peasant women in Syria, for instance, it was common for a woman to look after the children, make bread, get water, cut wood, milk the goats, and so on while her husband sat by. In Moslem societies where women walk several paces behind their husbands, a man could divorce his wife on a whim, leaving her destitute and cut off from her children. She had no redress. Ancient Near Eastern women were often shut out from society, forced behind curtains or veils. Most were illiterate, because some Middle Eastern people considered it a sin to teach a woman to read and to write. A woman had so little status in some societies, that if she received a letter, it would be addressed to her son, even if he were a babe in her arms!

Historians say that Hebrew women were a notable exception, however, for they were respected both at home and in society. Hebrew women mingled with men (Job's sons and daughters ate together—Job 1:4), pursued business outside the home (Proverbs 31:16), and were not always secluded from society, nor were they forced to wear a veil at all times. For instance, the Egyptians saw Sarah's face (Genesis 12:14), and Abraham's servant saw that Rebekeh was "very fair to look upon" (Genesis 24:15, 16).

Some women rose to high positions in commerce, government, or religion. In Old Testament times, Deborah ruled Israel (Judges 4 and 5), and the Bible lists a number of prophetesses, such as Miriam (Exodus 15:20), Deborah (Judges 4:4), Huldah (2 Kings 22:14), Noadiah (Nehemiah 6:14), and Anna (Luke 2:36). Women like Rahab, Esther, and Ruth also played significant roles in Israel's history—and in preserving the Christ line! While other cultures exclusively named sons as inheritors, the Mosaic Law made provisions for daughters to inherit (Numbers 27). Women also played a vital role in Jesus Christ's earthly ministry, as well as in the early church's. So while the picture of the insignificant, degraded woman might be of ancient Near Eastern origin, it isn't necessarily biblical.

At home, women were kept busy feeding and clothing their families (see chapters 2 and 3). Women laundered garments using a liquid soap made from wood ashes, by beating the dirt out with a stick, or by washing the garment in a running brook. Hebrew women taught their offspring the Torah, especially instructing daughters in the practical aspects of the Law. Women oversaw servants, tended flocks of sheep and goats, and sometimes participated in trade and commerce. In New Testament times, women sold cloth or dye, or offered services, such as weaving, spinning, or midwifery. Village women worked in the fields and cultivated fig and olive orchards.

Women went to the well daily to get fresh water, usually in the late afternoon or evening. Drawing water was a pleasant task, for at the well a woman could stop and fellowship with other townswomen. According to ancient Near Eastern custom, the well was also one of the few places where a woman could speak to a man in public. The man could ask for water for himself or his animals, but they couldn't converse. Jesus Christ's disciples were surprised when he spoke at length with the Samaritan woman at Jacob's well, for it countered the culture of the day (John 4:5-30). This tradition of women drawing the water is still carried on in parts of the Middle East today. Visitors to the Bible lands say it is a beautiful sight to see the women, dressed in brightly-colored robes, coming to and from the village well each night, carrying their earthenware jugs on their shoulders.

Search the Scriptures

When Ruth asked Boaz to place his "skirt" (mantle) over her, she was asking him to marry her. In the ancient Near East a mantle represented protection, and to marry a woman was also to redeem her (Ruth 3:9).

In the Near East, a woman's ten pieces of silver were given to her as a present from her betrothed husband. Although not worth much monetarily, these coins represented a husband's love and God's blessings on a marriage. If the girl lost one of these coins, it would be considered a disgrace. She would search diligently until the piece was recovered and would be thrilled when it was found. Jesus Christ compared this woman's joy to the joy in heaven whenever a sinner repents (Luke 15:8-10).

In the ancient Near East, weddings often took place in the evening. On the night before the wedding ceremony, ten girls (translated "virgins" in the King James Version) would meet the bridegroom with lamps or special torches at midnight. With their path lit, they would lead the groom and his relatives to the bride. Only a foolish girl would be unprepared to meet the groom. Jesus Christ used this illustration to warn his disciples to be prepared for his return (Matthew 25:1-13).

Betrothal

Dating as we know it didn't exist in biblical times, because older boys and girls were not permitted to mix socially. In the ancient Near East, marriages were arranged by the father, elders, or parents—often planned from the child's infancy. In some primitive Bedouin tribes, marriage was little more than a business transaction between two men. Women were considered chattel to be bought and sold at the best asking price. But among other ancient Near Eastern peoples, the marriage process was elaborate, well planned, and executed with consideration for the children's well being.

Customs varied in the ancient Near East, but generally a bride was chosen from among the groom's relatives—the same family or tribe. So it wasn't uncommon in biblical times for a man to marry his half-sister or cousin. Some type of inspection of the bridal candidate took place. For instance, the women of one family might visit the family of a certain marriageable daughter, feigning a social call. They would converse with their hosts, all the while scrutinizing the girl as she served them refreshments or a meal. The visitors evaluated not only the girl's physical qualities, but her attitude, too. Middle Easterners consider two qualities essential in a future bride: humility and a composed demeanor. A prideful or worrisome girl would be rejected, for they say such attitudes indicate a lack of trust in God. The inspection complete, the women returned home and reported to the father. If the girl was found suitable, the father would give her family a present to bind the agreement.

Sometimes a betrothal ceremony took place. Customs varied, but generally a betrothal ceremony would bring the two families together. The couple would sit facing one another. (The girl would be veiled.) The boy would then place into his future bride's hands ten pieces of silver—small coins stamped with the family's crest and the year. Although the coins weren't worth much monetarily, they were priceless for sentimental reasons. Middle Eastern people believe that love is kindled between the betrothed couple as soon as these silver pieces are dropped into the girl's hands. The couple then leaned forward until their foreheads touched. Placing a veil over their heads, a family elder pronounced a benediction.

Search the Scriptures

In the ancient Near East, kings or other wealthy men would provide wedding garments to their guests as a loving courteous gesture. To refuse to wear the wedding garment at the ceremony, therefore, would be an sult to the host—snubbing his kind provision (Matthew 22:11, 12).

In biblical times, the voices of the bride and bridegroom represented mirth and gladness (Jeremiah 7: 16:9; 33:11; John 3:29).

In Ephesians 5:37, the church is compared to a bride "not having spot, nor wrinkle." Girls who had wrinkle worry lines on their face were considered unsuitable brides because Near Eastern people believe this revea a lack of trust in God.

Marriage

In some Middle Eastern cultures both past and present, perhaps no event is more joyously anticipated than a wedding. Young girls are raised to look forward to that day as the pinnacle of their lives. So important is the wedding that virtually all other activities within the family cease. Those in mourning forestall their sorrow (Matthew 9:15), business transactions are put on hold, and travel is postponed. Even if the family is in the midst of another celebration, or if they are fasting (Mark 2:19), all must yield to the wedding festivities. Family, friends, and neighbors are all invited.

Historians tell us that in New Testament times, wedding celebrations typically lasted ten days. During that time the bride and groom stayed in their respective homes while family and friends attended them. Preparations for the bride alone took two days. She was bathed in perfumed water, and her hair was adorned with pearls and other jewels. On her wedding day, the bride was dressed in gorgeous scarlet garments embroidered with gold thread, and she was arrayed in glittering jewelry and other adornments (Revelation 21:2; Isaiah 61:10). Similarly, the bridegroom is specially bathed and dressed in wedding attire by his male relatives.

Some scholars say that weddings in the Gospel period usually took place in the groom's home. The wedding procession to his house was a momentous occasion. Dressed in her finery, the veiled bride walked under a linen canopy, upheld by her brothers or other male relatives. In the Middle East, the canopy represented God's protection. Family and friends flanked the streets as she passed, playing tambourines, shouting blessings, and throwing flowers in her path. Indeed, the whole town might come out to see the bride!

Once everyone was assembled in the groom's house, the doors were shut, and no one else was allowed in. (Evidently the doors were locked to keep out thieves and other intruders, for the house at this time would be filled with money, jewels, and other gifts for the couple.) Vows were exchanged. A salt covenant might be taken (see Chapter 2). In the ancient Near East, couples did not exchange wedding rings. Instead, the groom lifted off his bride's veil and placed it on his shoulder, symbolizing his promise to protect her. The married couple then walked together under the canopy to the wedding feast— often a days-long celebration filled with music, food, dancing, and laughter.

Honeymoon

In biblical times, newlyweds customarily took a yearlong "honeymoon." The Mosaic Law stipulated that during this twelve-month period, the man could not be sent off to war, nor could he be given business duties outside the family (Deuteronomy 24:5). Often during that year, the husband prepared a special apartment at his father's house for himself and his new wife. Before a new husband left for war or business, he would comfort his bride, assuring her of his love and of his speedy return. Perhaps this concept is present in Jesus' comforting words in John 14:1-3: "Let not your heart be troubled: ye believe in God, believe also in me. In my Father's house are many mansions: if it were not so, I would have told you. I go to prepare a place for you. And if I go and prepare a place for you, I will come again, and receive you unto myself; that where I am, there ye may be also."

Children

Ancient Near Eastern people considered children to be a blessing from God, and they desired large families: "Lo, children are an heritage of the Lord: and the fruit of the womb is his reward. As arrows are in the hand of a mighty man; so are children of the youth. Happy is the man that hath his quiver full of them: they shall not be ashamed, but they shall speak with the enemies in the gate" (Psalm 127:3-5).

A barren woman in biblical times was considered to be cursed or forsaken by God. In some cultures, childless women were social pariahs, denied pleasures like carrying offerings into the temple, attending weddings, or bestowing blessings on a bride or groom. Evidently this mindset continued from Old Testament times into the Gospel period, for both Rachel and Elisabeth said that God took away their shame after giving birth to sons (see Genesis 30:23; Luke 1:24, 25).

It's no secret that Middle Eastern women especially wanted sons. An Arabian proverb reflects this preference: "May the blessings of Allah be upon thee. May your shadows never grow less. May all your children be boys and not girls."

Historians say that some families celebrated the birth of sons, but not daughters. In the Gospel period, musicians customarily would wait outside the house of an expectant mother. If she delivered a son, they banged drums, played instruments, and shouted the good news in the streets, but they were silent if a daughter was born. "Wealth and sons are the ornaments of life," the Koran says—an attitude that prevails in most of the Middle East today.

This preference for boys stems in part from the fact that sons were essential to an agricultural society. In addition, sons added to the family's wealth while daughters detracted from it. A son could be expected to stay with his father, working with him at his trade. In many parts of the ancient Near East, when a son married, he brought his wife and her dowry (money and possessions) home with him. Their offspring were added to the father's family. Girls, on the other hand, departed from their fathers when married, taking their inheritance with them.

Near Eastern people were also interested in sons because they wanted to preserve the family line at all costs. The Hebrews certainly felt this way, for the Law of Moses required a man to marry his brother's widow with the express purpose of carrying on his family name (Deuteronomy 25:5-7). A Hebrew woman might have wanted a son for a very different reason: he could have been the promised Messiah!

It may be hard to imagine that under the Mosaic Law, disobedient and rebellious sons could be put to death (Deuteronomy 21:18-21), but in biblical times, children were expected to obey their parents and to respect their elders. A disobedient child was a terrible disgrace to his family, and open rebellion was generally not tolerated. As a mark of their respect, Middle Eastern children would respond immediately to their parent's call. Note how the boy Samuel, when he thought he heard Eli call, ran to the aged prophet (1 Samuel 3:5). A child might greet his father each morning by kissing his hand, then stand silently by, awaiting his command. Children routinely bowed down to greet their parents. Even after he was king, Solomon bowed down to greet his mother (1 Kings 2:19).

Salted and Swaddled

When sons of a certain status were born, they might be salted and swaddled—an ancient custom involving rubbing the baby with salt or salt water and wrapping him in strips of linen cloth. After he was washed with salt water, the baby was wrapped

from the neck down in linen strips, his arms bound by his side. (The type and color of the cloth reflected the family's station in life.) The baby was left in this position for a short time while the parents dedicated him to God. Because salt represented integrity, rubbing a baby with brine symbolized that the boy would be raised to speak and act truthfully. Constricting his body symbolized that he would be reared to live honestly before God.

In Hebrew households, male infants were circumcised on the eighth day. Babies were typically named on that day, too. According to custom, sons were given a family member's name or a name that described a characteristics of God. For instance, Abijah means "whose father God is" and Ahaziah means "held by Jehovah." When Elisabeth wanted to name her son "John," her family protested because it countered culture (see Luke 1:59-63). Girls might be named for beautiful things or pleasant characteristics, such as Rhoda (rose), Esther (star), Rachel (lamb), or Salome (peace).

Growing Up

In biblical times, a boy worked alongside his father learning his trade or profession. Jesus probably learned carpentry from Joseph (Mark 6:3). Boys were trusted with responsibility at an early age. By seventeen or eighteen, he might be a husband, a father, and an overseer of his own business or farm. In fact, historians estimate that the average man in Bible times was a father at nineteen, a grandfather at thirty-eight, and a great-grandfather at fifty-seven!

While boys were apprenticed to their fathers, girls learned domestic skills like cooking, spinning, and weaving from their mothers. By the time she was married (usually at puberty), a Near Eastern girl knew how to govern a home and care for children— no small feat in biblical times! A daughter was also responsible to keep oil lamps burning at home, and she might be a shepherdess over a small flock of sheep or goats. Socially, though, girls were sheltered. They were chaperoned in public and were forbidden to speak with men outside their own family. Even at social gatherings like weddings and feasts, girls stayed within a tight circle of female relatives (see Esther 1:5, 9).

Search the Scriptures

In Luke 2:12 the shepherds are told they would find the baby in swaddling clothes. These were the strips of linen used in the custom of salting and swaddling a baby. Scholars say that Mary probably washed the baby with salt water, too, for salting and swaddling were done together.

In Ezekiel 16:4 we read that Jerusalem was "not salted at all, nor swaddled at all." This is a derogatory statement meaning that the inhabitants of Jerusalem were not honest or trustworthy. To be salted and swaddled represented integrity of speech and of character.

Respect for Elders

A young boy running errands in Jerusalem

In the ancient Near East, families usually included grandparents, uncles, aunts, cousins, and possibly servants. Tent dwelling families camped together for protection. But in sedentary societies, families might live and work together for social and economic reasons. Women could help one another with children and household responsibilities, while men could farm and tend flocks together. The Middle Eastern view of family solidarity also factors in. A Middle Eastern man would not typically move away from his village or relatives. Only desperate circumstances, like famine or drought, would draw a man away from his kindred. According to the culture of the day, it was extraordinary that Abraham left his relatives and country to journey from Haran (Genesis 12:1-5).

In the Middle East, respect for elders is nearly universal. "He that is older than you by a day is wiser than you by a year," says an ancient Syrian proverb. The Mosaic Law commanded respect for the elderly: "Thou shalt rise up before the hoary head, and honour the face of the old man, and fear thy God: I am the Lord" (Leviticus 19:32).

Grandparents often took on advisory roles in the family. In New Testament times, Jewish grandfathers might assume their grandson's religious education for a while. At night, a grandfather would take his young grandson into bed with him to teach him the Scriptures. In the morning, the grandfather quizzed the boy to see what he had retained. These lessons were so important that a grandfather wouldn't interrupt them for anything. Jesus Christ possibly refers to this custom in the gospel of Luke: "And he from within shall answer and say, Trouble me not: the door is now shut, and my children are with me in bed; I cannot rise and give thee" (Luke 11:7).

Family Life

Search the Scriptures

Here is a list of Scriptures that mention various aspects of family life.

Household

Genesis 18:19
Genesis 35:2
Genesis 45:11,18
Genesis 47:12, 24
Deuteronomy 11:6
Deuteronomy 12:7
Joshua 2:18
Joshua 7:14, 18
Judges 6:27
Judges 18:25
1 Samuel 25:17
1 Samuel 27:3
2 Samuel 6:11
2 Samuel 15:16
1 Kings 5:9, 11
2 Kings 8:1, 2
Job 1:3
Proverbs 31:15, 21, 27
Acts 10:7
Romans 16:10, 11
Ephesians 2:19
Galatians 6:10

Well/Water

Genesis 21:19, 25
Genesis 24:11-43
Genesis 26:18-22
Genesis 29:1-12
1 Samuel 9:11
2 Samuel 23:15-17
Proverbs 10:11
Proverbs 20:5

Wed/Wedding

Ezekiel 16:38
Matthew 22:3-12
Luke 12:6
Luke 14:8

Bride/ Bridegroom

Psalm 19:5
Isaiah 49:18
Isaiah 61:10
Isaiah 62:5
Jeremiah 2:32
Jeremiah 7:34
Jeremiah 16:9
Jeremiah 25:10
Jeremiah 33:11
Joel 2:16
Matthew 9:15
Matthew 25:1-10
Mark 2:19, 20
Luke 5:34, 35
John 2:9
John 3:29
Revelation 18:23
Revelation 21:2, 9
Revelation 22:17

Banner

Psalm 60:4
Song of Solomon 2:4
Isaiah 13:2

Family

Leviticus 20:5
Leviticus 25:10-49
Numbers 3:21-33
Numbers 26:5-58
Numbers 27:4, 11
Numbers 36:6-12
Deuteronomy 29:18
Joshua 7:14, 17
Judges 6:15
Judges 9:1
Judges 13:2
Judges 17:7
Judges 18:2-19
Judges 21:24
Ruth 2:1
1 Samuel 9:21
1 Samuel 10:21
1 Samuel 18:18
1 Samuel 20:6, 29
2 Samuel 14:7
2 Samuel 16:5
1 Chronicles 4:27
1 Chronicles 6:61, 70, 71
1 Chronicles 13:14
Esther 9:28
Jeremiah 3:14
Jeremiah 8:3
Amos 3:1
Micah 2:3
Zechariah 12:12-14
Zechariah 14:18
Ephesians 3:15

Salting and Swaddling an Infant

Materials Needed:

- Doll, preferably the size and form of a newborn or infant
- ½ yard thin white cloth, like muslin
- scissors
- yard stick for measuring
- 1 teaspoon salt
- 1 cup warm water

Directions:

1. Prepare swaddling clothes by cutting about six strips 2 to 4 inches wide by 10 to 16 inches long. (Length doesn't have to be precise; it really depends on the size of the doll. Women likely tore the strips, anyway.)
2. Dissolve the salt in water.
3. Take a piece of material and "wash" the doll in salt water.
4. Wrap the swaddling clothes around the doll, starting at the neck and ending up at the feet being sure not to cover the face. Try to keep the doll's arms straight by its sides when wrapping.

   You can try the same thing on a real infant, provided, of course, that you have the parent's permission and supervision. Take special care not to cover the baby's face when wrapping him, and don't get salt water in his eyes.

"Whose Task Is It?" Game

Based on information from this chapter, match up the tasks listed below with the appropriate family member. Keep in mind that there may be more than one member for some tasks.

Family Members:
- Mother
- Father
- Son
- Daughter

Tasks:
- Grind grain
- Arrange marriages
- Get water
- Cook food
- Judge a dispute
- Tend goats
- Tend sheep
- Tend camels or oxen
- Tend a garden
- Harvest
- Plow the field
- Winnow grain
- Clean laundry
- Make beds
- Sweep floor
- Dig a cistern
- Provide a dowry
- Sit in the gates
- Get kindling
- Make a fire
- Churn butter
- Weave thread
- Erect a tent
- Teach the Ten Commandments
- Go to synagogue school
- Learn the family trade

Ten Pieces of Silver

Materials Needed:

- a quarter or half dollar
- pencil, marker, etc.
- cardboard
- silver spray paint
- scissors
- small paper clips
- bandanna (optional)

Directions:

1. Spray cardboard with silver paint on both sides.
2. Trace ten circles the size of a quarter or half dollar on the cardboard and cut them out.
3. On one side of each coin, write the year. On other side, draw a family crest.
4. Punch a small hole in the top of each coin and attach a paper clip to each of the silver pieces.
5. Tie a piece of twine or a bandanna around your head, then attach the ten pieces of silver to the bandanna.

You can act out a betrothal ceremony with these ten pieces of silver. Have boy and girls sit on the floor, opposite one another. The boy places the ten pieces of silver into the girls cupped hands. The couple lean towards each other with foreheads touching, and the elder, or priest places a thin veil over the heads of the couple while he gives his blessing. Middle Eastern people believe that as soon as the man places the ten pieces of silver into the girl's hands, their love becomes kindled.

Bridal Canopy

Materials Needed:

- four poles, about 3 feet long (½-inch dowels will work well)
- 3-foot-wide by 5-foot-long piece of muslin or other material
- string
- tassels (optional)

Directions:

1. If you are using tassels, sew them on four sides of fabric, evenly spaced.

2. Tie the poles to the four corners of the fabric with string. Be sure to overlap enough fabric so that about 6 inches hang down on four sides.

Have a boy and girl act as bride and groom. Have other children carry the bridal canopy over the couple.

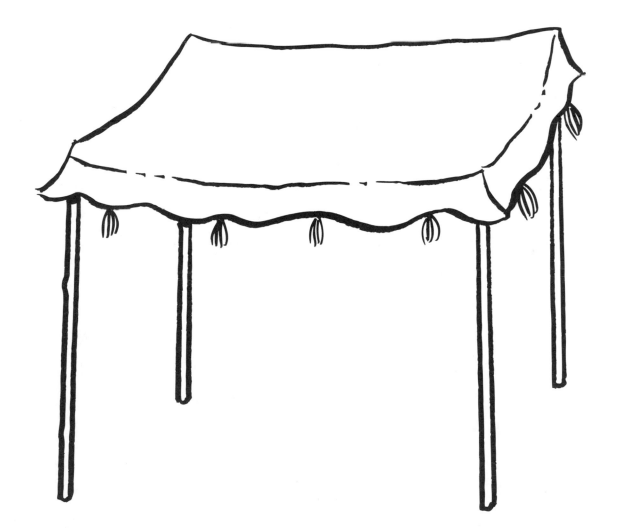

The Name Game

In the word search puzzle below, try to find the Bible names listed in the left column. Then try to match the names with their meanings in the right column.

Men of the Bible

Abijah	Supplanter
Ahaziah	Whom God Created
Azariah	My God Is Jehovah
Obadiah	Servant of Jehovah
Daniel	Whose Father God Is
Elijah	God Will Strengthen
Elkanah	Held by Jehovah
Ezekiel	Rest
Noah	Helped by Jehovah
Isaac	Laughter
Jacob	God Is My Judge

Women of the Bible

Jemima	Gazelle
Tabitha	Dove
Dorcas	Star
Rhoda	Rose
Rachel	Gazelle
Salome	Lamb
Esther	Princess
Sarah	Peace

```
Z T A B I J A H K L H M E L I J H A
J E L K A N A H R A H N S J S O M S
A I U L I V A D A J E M I M A N I A
H A N A S B D A N I E L O I S A E L
C Z R H O D A H A E L I J A H A A O
L A E O B A D I A H N K D E H N B M
K R E S T I E S T H E R A O O S I E
R I X Z T A B I T H A L E A R A G I
W A S U E K T N O A E B H A A C L H
S H V A F K S S O A H A Z I A H A N
T R B R R I I J R A C H E L M O S
O M L N W A N E L H U L I M Y S T S
Z I S A A C H V L Y A J A C O B A X
```

The Name Game

Answers

Men of the Bible

Abijah — Supplanter
Ahaziah — Whom God Created
Azariah — My God Is Jehovah
Obadiah — Servant of Jehovah
Daniel — Whose Father God Is
Elijah — God Will Strengthen
Elkanah — Held by Jehovah
Ezekiel — Rest
Noah — Helped by Jehovah
Isaac — Laughter
Jacob — God Is My Judge

Women of the Bible

Jemima — Gazelle
Tabitha — Dove
Dorcas — Star
Rhoda — Rose
Rachel — Gazelle
Salome — Lamb
Esther — Princess
Sarah — Peace

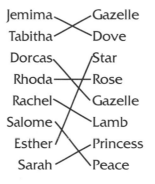

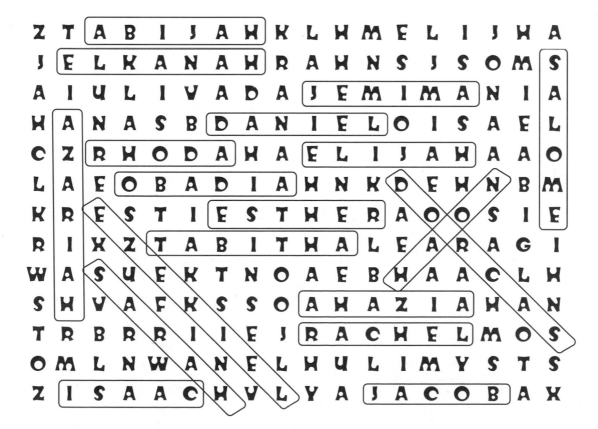

Chapter Six

Farms, Fields, and Marketplaces

"Caleb—wake up, " Simon whispered. He stood over his older brother and gently prodded him with his staff. "Even chief shepherds cannot escape the night watch, brother."

Caleb got to his feet, ignoring his brother's teasing. Rubbing the sleep from his eyes, Caleb picked up his thick cloak, shook it out, and then slipped his arms through the sleeves. A coyote howled in the distance.

"We'll need to build up the fire tonight, Simon." Caleb said, tying a belt around his waist. "Help me gather brush before you retire."

The men worked quietly so that they wouldn't awaken the other shepherds. Soon the fire blazed, casting a soft light on the herd of sheep huddled together in their bramble pen. The animals were asleep. Simon took off his cloak and spread it out near the other shepherds who were snoring by the fire.

"That coyote won't keep me awake tonight, but these snoring lions will," Simon said as he settled down to sleep. Caleb laughed. Within minutes, Simon's snoring drowned out the rest of the men.

Caleb looked up into the black sky dotted with stars. He liked these solitary night watches—they were quiet and peaceful. He sat down in the doorway of the pen and listened to the even breathing of the sheep. *It is a good flock—healthy and strong,* Caleb thought. He listened for the coyote but heard only the fire crackling nearby. *It will be a peaceful night.*

Laying his staff down, Caleb took the scrip out of his belt. He unwrapped his dinner: a barley loaf, some olives, and a wedge of cheese. Caleb prayed aloud, "Thank you, Lord God Almighty, from whom all good things come. Amen." He liked to pray out loud to God on these night watches and to sing psalms of praise to him out under the starry sky.

Finished with his meal, Caleb looked up at the winking stars. Now came his favorite game—naming the constellations. Caleb had progressed to the western-most sky when out of nowhere, a man appeared. Caleb jumped to his feet! His heart pounded in his chest and he opened his mouth to call out, but no words would come. He wanted to reach for his staff, but he could not move for the man before him shone with brilliance, a light so beautiful and so powerful it illuminated the sheepcote and the surrounding meadows. All the shepherds were awake now, trembling with fear as the angel spoke:

"Fear not: for, behold, I bring you good tidings of great joy, which shall be to all people. For unto you is born this day in the city of David a Savior, which is Christ the Lord."

Caleb fell prostrate on the earth.

"And this shall be a sign unto you," the angel continued. "Ye shall find the babe wrapped in swaddling clothes, lying in a manger."

Immediately, the shepherds heard a multitude of voices, like the shout of an army, praising God and saying,

" Glory to God in the highest, and on earth peace, good will toward men."

Then as suddenly as the angels appeared, they were gone.

"The angel of the Lord!" Caleb exclaimed, scrambling to his feet.

"Did you hear him?" shouted another. "He said the Messiah is born!"

"Yes—it is the Christ! The Christ!" another cried, tears streaming down his face.

Caleb stilled their cheers. He needed time to think, to make sense of the wondrous words. Was it true? Was the long-awaited for Messiah really born this day? The others crowded around him expectantly.

"What should we do, Caleb?" they asked.

"We must go to the city of David at once," he answered. "And search for a baby in swaddling clothes."

"To Bethlehem! To Bethlehem!" the shepherds cheered. And they ran towards the city with Caleb leading the way, singing praises aloud to God as he went.

The Bible is filled with farming terminology, like the seed and sower, the vine and branches, and reaping what you sow. To the predominantly

agricultural society of the ancient Near East, such illustrations would have been readily understood. When John the Baptist said Jesus would come "with a fan in his hand," listeners knew he was talking about a winnowing fork, used to separate grain from chaff. When Jesus told Peter that Satan desired to sift him like wheat (Luke 22:31), Peter would have gotten the picture! Understanding ancient farming methods and customs, therefore, helps shed light on many passages in the Bible.

Seed Time and Harvest

In the Palestine area, the farming season started around October or November after the early rains, or "former rains," had softened the sun-hardened ground. Using his simple wooden plow attached to a team of oxen, the farmer churned up his fields, sowing seeds as he went. Barley and wheat were his two main crops, followed by beans, lentils, and other legumes. In the early spring, the "latter rains" again watered his fields. The Near Eastern farmer combated many enemies including hail, hot desert winds, locusts and other pests, as well as hostile tribesmen who might set his fields on fire or plant tares among his grain. Tares closely resemble wheat but yield a black, poisonous kernel (Matthew 13:24-30).

If the farmer outwitted his enemies, his crops were ready for harvest, starting with barley in early spring. Farmers cut the grain with sickles, bound it into sheaves, and transported it by mule or donkey to the threshing floor. According to the Mosaic Law, farmers were to leave a portion of their fields for the gleaners—widows, strangers, and other people who might need food (Leviticus 23:22; Deuteronomy 24:19-22). Custom also permitted people to eat the grains as they hardened on the stalk but not to carry any away with them. In the Gospels, Jesus Christ and his disciples followed this custom. The Pharisees reproved them, not for helping themselves to the grain, but for doing so on the Sabbath (Matthew 12:1, 2; Mark 2:23, 24; Luke 6:1, 2).

Search the Scriptures

In Acts 26:14, Jesus Christ tells Paul it is "hard for thee to kick against the pricks." This refers to the goads or pointed sticks farmers used to prod their oxen forward. Sometimes, an ox would kick back at the goad, but the farmer would only hold the instrument at the animal's heels, forcing the animal forward. The inference is that it was difficult for Saul to avoid the will of God.

Mixed animals were forbidden to plow together (Deuteronomy 22:10) not only because the furrows might be uneven, but also because the stronger animal might hurt the weaker. Likewise, Christian believers are not to be unequally yoked together with unbelievers (2 Corinthians 6:14).

Threshing and Winnowing

Harvested grains were transported to the threshing floor—a hardened, well-drained patch of ground situated to catch the prevailing winds. To thresh grain (separate the kernel from the plant), the farmer spread out sheaves on the floor then guided his oxen so they could trample the grain.

After the threshing process had removed the grain from the stalk, the winnowing process separated the grain from the useless chaff. Winnowing was typically done in the evening, when the winds had picked up. Using a large wooden fork called a winnowing fan (which looked like a pitchfork), the farmer tossed the chopped mixture into the air. The heavy grains fell to the ground while the lighter chaff blew away by the wind and was later burned. A sieve was used for a final sifting (see Matthew 3:12). During the busy harvest season, farmers like Boaz in the book of Ruth often camped out on the threshing floor to guard against thieves. Harvest was a joyous time for Near Eastern people (Isaiah 9:3).

Search the Scriptures

The Law forbade oxen to be muzzled as they trampled grain in the threshing process (Deuteronomy 25:4). References to this are made in the New Testament, indicating that ministers are entitled to make a living preaching the gospel (1 Corinthians 9:7-14; 1 Timothy 5:18).

Isaiah 1:3 tells how oxen and asses know their masters. In Middle Eastern villages, a boy would put everyone's animals out to pasture in the morning. In the evening, he'd bring the animals to the edge of the village, and the animals would walk home by themselves, each one returning to its proper owner. While animals are smart enough to know to whom to return, Israel was not wise enough to return to God.

Vineyards

Experts say that a wide variety of grapes once grew in the Palestine area. Isaiah 5:1, 2 describes a typical Middle Eastern vineyard. Situated on a hill free of stones (terrace farming was popular in biblical times because of the hilly terrain), the vineyard was fenced in to keep out foxes and other thieves, and a watchtower and winepress were built within the enclosure. According to Law of Moses, travelers could eat grapes as they passed by, but they could not take any away with them (Deuteronomy 23:24). The Law also made provisions for gleaners (Leviticus 19:10).

At harvest time, grapes were processed in a winepress—a shallow pit lined with stone and mortar, like a cistern, which had collecting bins stationed below to catch the juice. The fruit was pulverized by rolling a stone around the press, or it was trodden underfoot by barefooted men and women. The liquid was drunk as juice or made into wine.

In biblical times, making wine was simple. Grape juice was set out in the sun for about six weeks then left undisturbed in clay jugs for another forty days. (Too much motion can turn fermented grape juice into vinegar.) During that time, twigs, stems, and other sediment fell to the bottom of the jug. Finally, the wine was carefully poured into a new wineskin or jug and sealed with wax with the family's name inscribed on the sealant.

Other grape by-products included raisins and dibs—the thick syrup remaining after water in grape juice had boiled away. This golden syrup was extremely sweet and was used in place of honey. Wine and myrrh were mixed together and used as a painkiller, possibly the drink offered to Jesus Christ in Matthew 27:34.

In September when grapes were usually harvested, the whole village might move to the vineyard. There would be singing, dancing, and celebration (Judges 9:27). In the ancient Near East, grapevines were associated with a settled life—possibly because grapes take a long time to grow and produce fruit. Nearly every household would have a few vines. Grapes and vines were popular motifs in ancient Near Eastern art, for the fruit was also symbolic for prosperity, joy, and security, as is indicated in 1 Kings 4:25: "And Judah and Israel dwelt safely, every man under his vine and under his fig tree, from Dan even to Beer-sheba, all the days of Solomon."

Olives and Figs

Dark-barked, gnarled olive trees once dominated the Palestinian countryside. These long-lived trees (some that remain today reportedly go back to the days of Christ) required little cultivation and yielded a prolific amount of fruit—olives from one tree can make twenty gallons of oil! Olives were harvested last in the season, usually by boys and women. They shook the trees or beat them with long poles, catching the tiny

Ripe figs

fruit in baskets. During harvest, gleaners were given access to olive trees, as the Mosaic Law required (Deuteronomy 24:20). The finest olives were pressed into beaten oil, which was reserved for use in the Temple. Whole olives were stored in salt water, but the majority of the fruit was pressed into oil and stored in clay jars or goatskin bottles. The oil replaced butter in cooking, and it fueled clay lamps. Men rubbed the perfumed oil into their beards, and women used it to soften their face and hair. The thick oil was used for medicinal purposes and to preserve leather. In ancient cultures, olives and olive branches symbolized peace and rest.

Fig trees were also commonplace in the lands and times of the Bible. This tree can grow upwards of thirty feet and yields two or three crops per year. Like olive trees, fig trees required little care and were ordinarily cultivated by women. After the winter rains, fig trees produced small edible buds. Later in the spring, they produced mature fruit, most of which fell to the ground or was harvested. In August or September, a second, larger crop grew. While most figs were for immediate eating, some were pressed into cakes or were dried and stored. Throughout the Near East, this sprawling tree was enjoyed for its shade. Symbolically, it represented security and prosperity (1 Kings 4:25).

Search the Scriptures

In the Middle East, grape harvest was a joyous time filled with singing, shouting, and dancing. When Jeremiah foretells of desolation, he says winepresses will fail and shouting will cease (Jeremiah 48:33). To the ancient Near Easterner, a dry winepress and a silent grape harvest was a picture of sadness indeed!

Another picture of desolation was an abandoned cottage in a vineyard (Isaiah 1:8). This was the temporary shelter built in the vineyard, which was left to decay when grape harvest ended. The ramshackle hut was quickly blown apart by the winds.

Psalm 128:3 speaks of olive sprouts. These are the little plants that grow at the base of the tree, giving it support as it ages. Middle Eastern people believe that children are to support their parents in their old age; otherwise, they are considered infidels, unfaithful to their family and to their beliefs.

Isaiah 55:1 speaks of buying wine and water without money. According to ancient custom, a person gave presents to others on his birthday rather than receiving them. Therefore, he might go to the market on his birthday and buy wine or milk to give away. Paying the merchant in secret, he would say, "Announce to everyone to come and drink for free."

Sheep and Shepherds

The Bible abounds with references to sheep and shepherds. Abraham, Abel, Jacob, Amos, and David were once shepherds, and so was Moses before he led the Israelites out of captivity (Exodus 3:1). News of the Messiah's birth was delivered first to "shepherds abiding in the field" (Luke 2:8, 9). For most Near Eastern people, sheep and shepherds were a part of everyday life. When the Psalmist said a good shepherd leads his sheep by still waters, Middle Easterners would know why—sheep are too timid to drink at a running brook. When the Bible compares God to a loving shepherd, ancient Near Easterners could relate!

In ancient times, a man's wealth was often tied up in his flocks. For instance, the Bible says that Abraham was "very rich in cattle, in silver, and in gold" (Genesis 13:2), and that Job, "the greatest of all the men of the East," owned at least 14,000 sheep (Job 42:12). King Solomon had such fortunes that he sacrificed 120,000 of these animals at the dedication of the Temple (1 Kings 8:63). Wealthy men would hire out shepherds to care for their immense flocks. Villages might designate a few shepherds to look after all the animals in the community.

A shepherd's life was often lonely and dangerous. He spent long hours away from home, protecting his flock from thieves, wolves, bears, and other enemies. (Sheep have no natural defense against predators and hardly resist when attacked.) Typically, Middle Eastern shepherds were knowledgeable of animal husbandry and of astronomy, as they spent many nights out in the open fields. A good shepherd cherished his flocks, sometimes knowing each animal by name. In turn, the sheep would respond only to the shepherd's voice.

Middle Eastern shepherds don't drive their animals from behind like other herdsmen, but gently lead them instead. If an animal were lost, a shepherd searched diligently for the animal, for his reputation was at stake—a shepherd would be disgraced if he lost one animal (see Matthew 18:12). At night when predators lurked, the shepherd herded his flock into a cave for safekeeping, or fenced them in using stones or brambles. The shepherd lay down at the opening to the enclosure, acting as a doorway to the sheepfold. This image comes to mind when we read, "Then said Jesus unto them again, 'Verily, verily, I say unto you, I am the door of the sheep. All that ever came before me are thieves and robbers: but the sheep did not hear them. I am the door: by me if any man enter in, he shall be saved, and shall go in and out, and find pasture.... I am the good shepherd: the good shepherd giveth his life for the sheep'" (John 10:7-11).

Rod and Staff

A shepherd typically carried with him a sling, scrip, staff, and rod. If an animal went astray, the shepherd used his sling to toss a stone in front of the animal's nose. The startled animal then quickly rejoined the flock. Slings were used for accuracy as well as for distance. An Arabian proverb says: "A habitual liar is one who puts a secret in a sling," meaning that falsehoods travel far. With his club-like rod, the shepherd warded off approaching enemies. With his staff or large pole the shepherd controlled and counted the sheep as they passed into the sheepfold, marking every tenth animal as a tithe (Leviticus 27:31-33). The shepherd also carried a scrip, a small leather purse, to carry food and possibly a reed flute.

Sheep provided people with wool and meat, and their milk was made into yogurt and cheese. Typically, Middle Eastern people are fond of sheep, often treating them as beloved pets. These gentle, obedient animals are wholly dependent on a shepherd to lead, to protect, and to provide for them. They are easily startled and scatter when attacked. Unlike other animals, sheep do not ordinarily fight among themselves, but instead eat, sleep, and live peacefully.

In the Old Testament, God's people are compared to sheep (Psalm 44:22; 74:1; 78:52; 79:13; 95:7; 100:3), disobedient Israel is likened to scattered sheep, and unfaithful leaders are sometimes compared to irresponsible shepherds (Isaiah 53:6; Jeremiah 50:6, 17; Ezekiel 34:6-12).

In the New Testament, God's people are called the flock of God (1 Peter 5:2, 3), leaders are called pastors, which is another name for shepherds (Ephesians 4:11), and Jesus Christ is called the chief shepherd (1 Peter 5:4).

Goats and sheep often grazed together, but unlike docile sheep, goats are known to be destructive, mischievous, and headstrong, quick to fight among

Search the Scriptures

Psalm 23:1-5 compares God to a shepherd. A good shepherd finds green pastures for his sheep where the animals can rest while they graze. Milk production increases when sheep can graze unhurriedly. He waters them at still water supplies because sheep are too timid to drink from a running brook. When a Middle Easterner is exhausted and thirsty, he says his "soul has departed" from him. A good shepherd "restores the soul" of his sheep, meaning that he provides the animals with adequate water and rest. He leads his flock through safe passages. He quiets them as they walk through the dark, treacherous paths that wind between steep cliffs ("valley of the shadow of death") where bandits lurked in dark corners. A shepherd's rod and staff were used to protect the sheep from attackers.

themselves. While they provided people with many things—meat, milk, and hides for bottles, tents, and clothing—goats were generally disliked in some ancient Near Eastern cultures primarily because of their association with devils and idolatry among pagan nations. (For example, one of the principle gods of ancient Egypt, Mendes, was worshiped in the form of a goat.) In the ancient Near East, the goat was frequently compared to the devil. Out of this association arose a superstition. Some ancient Near Eastern people believed that if a sheep crossed their path, it meant good fortune, but a goat crossing portended bad. Considering these beliefs, it's no wonder Jesus made the comparison between goats and sheep in Matthew 25.

Skilled Craftsmen

If a man didn't make a living as a farmer or herdsman, he might be a craftsman, particularly if he lived in a city. A large metropolis in biblical times might employ any number of potters, carpenters, masons, doctors, weavers, as well as workers in leather, silver, and copper. Historians say that by New Testament times, craftsmen had developed mass production methods and were protected by trade guilds.

Potters

Pottery has ancient origins, but historians say that the Israelites never developed expertise in this field. To make earthenware objects—bowls, pitchers, lamps, and even toy figurines—the potter first mixed clay with water and limestone. With the vessel rest-

ing on a central axle, the potter turned his wheel by foot, shaping the vessel by hand. In the Old Testament, Israel is often described as clay fashioned by the potter's hand: "But now, O Lord, thou art our Father; we are the clay, and thou our potter; and we all are the work of thy hand" (Isaiah 64:8).

Once formed, the object was set aside to dry. Sometimes craftsmen decorated their work by scratching the surface with a hard object, or they painted it with red or black paint. (Archaeologists can date a pot by its shape and design alone.) The pot was then fired in a kiln, or underground oven. These fragile vessels were easily broken, but the frugal people of the East used the pieces (called "potsherds" in the King James Version) for scoops to carry water or hot coals. In the Bible, pending judgment is sometimes compared to shattering pots (see examples in Psalm 2:9; Jeremiah 19:10, 11; Revelation 2:27). Potsherds were used to scrape skin sores because the clay supposedly has medicinal properties (see Job 2:8)

Carpenters

In biblical times, carpentry was not for the faint of heart—or limb. Because all their work was done by hand, from felling trees to squaring limbs to making chariot wheels, carpenters needed brute strength, physical endurance, and manual dexterity to ply their trade. Isaiah describes the diverse skills of the carpenter (Isaiah 44:13, 14). The Bible says that Jesus Christ was a carpenter (Mark 6:3), so he probably was strong and muscular like other woodworkers of the time, and not the weak, emaciated figure often depicted in art. Historians say that the Israelites probably learned carpentry from the Phoenicians, who were experts in the field. In biblical times, carpenters made items like doors, window lattice, and crude furniture, such as stools, tables, and chests. They supplied farmers with yokes, plows, shovels, and winnowing fans, and they made carriages and wheels for charioteers. A carpenter's tool bench included simple tools like a saw, adze (cutting tool used to shape wood), hammer, pliers, vise, and file.

A grape/olive crusher

Stone Masons

Like carpentry, stone masonry required brute strength as well as skill. Masons preferred to chisel limestone in the quarry, then transport it to the work site. Solomon's temple was built in this manner though not for this reason (see 1 Kings 6:7). In addition to public buildings and city walls, masons built stone bridges, aqueducts, silos, wells, and cisterns. Architecturally, masons relied on cornerstones—four large, square rocks that gave the edifice strength and direction. Stone masons carefully selected the chief cornerstone, for all the lines of the building were determined from this one piece. In the ancient Near East, a chief cornerstone became a metaphor for a prominent, stable man in society. Jesus Christ is called the chief cornerstone in Acts 4:11, Ephesians 2:20, and 1 Peter 2:6, 7.

Metal Workers

Genesis 4:22 records the first mention of a metal worker, Tubal-cain, a worker in "brass and iron." Historians say that the earliest metal workers probably used gold first, a material that melts at low temperatures and is easily refined. Gold was fashioned into jewelry or was beaten into sheets for overlay work. Thin strips were cut to make gold thread. Less costly silver was used mostly in jewelry, and candlesticks, cups, and other pieces were also fashioned from silver. More mundane items like kettles, spears, and weaponry would be made out of copper, iron, and bronze.

In New Testament times, master metalsmiths set the standards for their industry and often held influential positions in commerce and in government. Demetrius, the chief silversmith in Ephesus in the apostle Paul's day, exerted considerable influence in that city (Acts 19:24, 25). Trade guilds were commonplace. To help one another in their profession, craftsmen typically lived and worked together in the same city quarters (see Acts 18:1-3).

Tanners

People who worked with leather were called tanners. They made tents, bottles, belts, helmets, shoes, and other items from goatskins and camel hides. (Sheepskin was too delicate for most purposes.) Processing hides was nasty, smelly work. Once the hair was scraped off, the skin was soaked in a mixture of sumac leaves, water, a bitter concoction from the oak tree, and dog manure. Because of the awful smell, tanneries were located outside the city—preferably down wind! The house of Simon the tanner, who is mentioned in Acts 10:6, was located near the sea, probably because of the smell but most likely because of the great need for water in the tanning process.

Fishermen cleaning their nets

Marketplace

A potter, carpenter, or other craftsman could sell his goods in the marketplace, which was usually located outside the main city gate or along a busy thoroughfare. Markets were exciting places filled with commotion. Merchants sat at their booths hawking everything from fresh produce to linen cloth to brass lamp stands. Ships brought in exotic animals like apes and peacocks, and herdsmen selling sheep and goats for sacrifices completed the menagerie. According to Middle Eastern custom, buyer and seller must haggle over the price of every item, from the most expensive tapestry to a cup of rice. "Two pieces of silver for the wool cloak," a buyer might say. "Why should I be concerned with money? I care only for your welfare—take it for nothing," the merchant facetiously replies, and on the dispute goes, sometimes erupting into a heated argument. The buyer degrades the item while the seller praises its worth. Proverbs 20:14 describes this type of exchange: "It is naught, it is naught, saith the buyer: but when he is gone his way, then he boasteth."

Ezekiel 27 paints a vivid picture of what these colorful bazaars looked like in biblical times. With majestic ships in port, traders in Tyrus (or Tyre) bartered their emeralds, white wool, brass, spices, cedar chests, livestock, and dozens of other items. In the marketplace you'd find poor people begging and unemployed men hunting for work, as well as travelers filling goatskin bottles with water—and their ears with gossip. Elders were greeted as they passed through the throngs on market day. Besides providing a backdrop for commerce, the marketplace also gave speakers a forum for debate, like the apostle Paul who disputed "in the market daily with them that met with him" (Acts 17:17).

Fruit vendors near the Damascus Gate, Jerusalem

Freshly picked olives

Crowded marketplace at the Damascus Gate

Winnowing Fork

Materials Needed:

- 4 craft sticks
- glue (hot glue gun preferred)
- 1 cup popcorn kernels
- 4 cups shredded newspaper or confetti
- an electric fan (optional)

Directions:

1. To make the fork, glue the craft sticks together as shown in diagram.
2. Mix the popcorn and confetti together and pour the mixture on a table.
3. Set up the fan so that it blows over the mixture you will be sifting.
4. To practice "winnowing," sift through the mixture. The lighter "chaff" will blow away, and the heavier "grains" will fall to the ground.

Classroom Ideas

1. Study John 10 noting the references to sheep and shepherds. How is Jesus Christ a "good shepherd?" Cite the verses.

2. List all the items mentioned in Ezekiel 27. Draw these items or cut pictures of them out of magazines and paste in a "marketplace."

3. Read through the book of Psalms, noting the references to sheep and shepherd. How is God like a shepherd? How is Israel like sheep?

4. Visit a sheep farm. What characteristics do sheep have? What methods do they use today to shepherd flocks? Has the relationship between shepherd and sheep changed since biblical times?

5. Visit a shop that makes pottery by hand.

6. Visit a weaver who spins and weaves by hand.

7. The Hearthsong Catalogue has many materials for the crafts in this chapter as well as many others. You can order a catalog at 800-325-2502 or by visiting their website at www.hearthsong.com.

Sling

This type of sling has ancient origins and likely would be made from leather.

Materials Needed:

- a 4-inch-by-28-inch strip of leather or vinyl
- scissors
- aluminum foil (enough to make a few "stones")

Directions:

1. Cut the material according to the shape of the accompanying diagram.
2. Stitch a small loop at one end of the material.
3. To use the sling, put one finger in the loop and grasp the other tapered end in the same hand making a large loop.
4. Place an aluminum foil "stone" in the center cup. (Remember David used a sling like this when he killed Goliath. It is not a toy. It can be dangerous and even deadly.)
5. Keeping your surroundings in mind, carefully spin the sling vertically at your side (sort of like a fast-pitch softball movement), letting go when you have obtained enough force to propel the "stone" at your target.

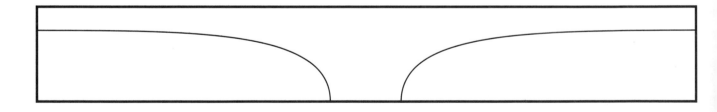

Make a Clay Pitcher

Materials Needed:

- modeling clay (preferably DAS terra-cotta)
- a sharp object (such as a stone, shell, or stick)

Directions:

1. Following directions for the clay, shape into a pitcher.
2. Decorate as the ancients would, by carving patterns in the moist clay using a sharp stone or shell.

Weaving a Mat

Materials Needed:

- 12-inch-by-10-inch piece of cloth
- 9-inch-by-13-inch piece of cloth (contrasting color)
- scissors
- ruler
- chalk, pen, or pencil
- needle and thread or hot-glue gun

Directions:

1. Using the ruler and chalk, mark eleven parallel lines about 1 inch apart on the larger piece of cloth. Make sure that you do not mark the lines all the way to the edge of the cloth; leave about ½ inch on each side.

2. Cut along the lines being careful not to cut to the ends of the cloth.

3. Cut the smaller piece of cloth into nine 1-inch-wide strips that are 13 inches long.

4. Begin weaving the strips through the slits cut in the other piece of cloth, alternating going over and under.

5. When you have woven a strip from one side to the other of the cloth, try to even up the ends so that there is an equal amount of the strip sticking out of both sides of the mat. You can then fold over the excess and either stitch it or glue it in place.

6. Start the next strip on the other side so that your mat will have a checkerboard appearance. Continue weaving all strips into the mat alternating directions.

7. When all the strips have been woven into the mat, you can secure each piece by stitching or gluing it in place.

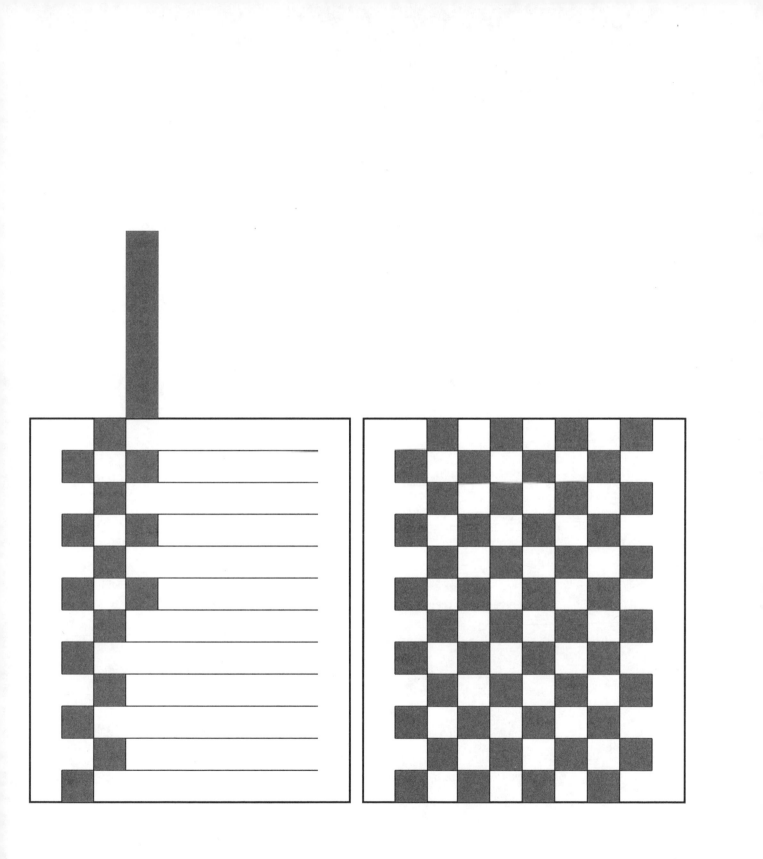

Chapter Seven

Toys, Games, Music, and Dance

"I will be glad and rejoice in thee: I will sing praise to thy name, O thou most High" (Psalm 9:2).

It was a perfect day to go to market in Jerusalem, sunny, cool, and not too windy. Deborah and her sister in-law, Dinah called to their children who were playing out in the courtyard.

"Ruth, Keriah—get the children ready," Dinah said.

Eleven year-old Ruth, the oldest of the children, helped lace the sandals of the little ones—her brothers, Samuel and Benjamin, and her young cousins Abigail and Nathaniel.

"Keriah—bring along that small mat near the cistern. We'll need it," Ruth ordered. She turned to a tall, ten-year-old boy. "And Micah, run and get your flute, or we'll have nothing to do at market."

"Bossy hen!" Micah teased, as he ran into the house to fetch his instrument.

"What's that in your hand?" Ruth asked little Benjamin. He stretched out his chubby fingers, revealing a tiny wooden sheep.

"My lambie," the three-year-old answered.

Ruth smiled at him. He always seemed to have some little toy in his hand. "All right, bring him along too."

Deborah and Dinah, baskets in hand, came into the courtyard.

"Are you all ready?" Deborah asked, surveying the group.

"Yes!" they answered. The band of seven children skipped behind their mothers as they walked down the dusty road to Jerusalem.

By the time they reached the ancient walled city, the market was thick with people: vendors and buyers, herdsmen selling animals for sacrifice, travelers from around the world, and children of all ages running and laughing in the streets. Deborah led the children to an open area by the city wall.

"Play here by the sheep gate, " Deborah instructed. "Ruth, mind the herdsmen and keep a sharp eye on the little ones. Your mother and I will be back soon. Shalom!"

"Shalom!" they answered.

With their mothers out of sight, the younger children huddled around the Ruth.

"What shall we play?" Keriah asked.

"What about wedding? I shall be the bride," Abigail offered.

"Let's play funeral," Samuel said. "We played wedding last time."

"No, let's be Gideon and the Midianites! The sword of the Lord and Gideon!" ten-year-old Micah shouted, brandishing his imaginary sword.

"No, there aren't enough of us for that, Micah," Ruth answered. "Let's play wedding. First, we'll have the dance. Micah, can you play that lively tune Uncle Reuben taught you?"

Ruth, Keriah, and Abigail linked arms and danced while Micah played a spirited tune on his reed pipe. The other boys sat cross-legged on the ground, watching disinterestedly. Samuel traced pictures in the dirt with his finger. "Are you done being married yet?" asked four year-old Nathaniel.

"I can see that my brothers take no joy in this wedding," Ruth said. "Shall we play funeral instead? Who wants to be a mourner?"

All raised their hands.

"You can't all be mourners. Someone needs to pretend to be dead," Ruth said.

"I'll do it!" Abigail and Nathaniel exclaimed together.

"No, let me do it, Ruth. Abigail was dead last time," Samuel argued.

Three-year-old Benjamin pushed his way past his brother and cousins.

"Me! Me! Me!" he said, tugging on Ruth's tunic.

"All right little lamb—lie down on this." Ruth spread the small mat out on the ground. She knelt down beside Benjamin and whispered in his ear. "You must lie very still, like you're sleeping." Benjamin giggled, then closed his eyes tightly. Micah played a slow, melancholy tune, and the others gathered around. The girls cried mock tears, each trying to out-wail the other, while the boys solemnly shook their heads. Delighted

with the effect, Benjamin sat up and cheered, "Hurrah! Hurrah!"

"Benny! You can't do that—lie down!" Abigail scolded.

"Oh, this is foolish," Micah interrupted. He tucked his flute into his belt and pulled out a small leather pouch. "Let's play marbles. Everyone stand behind this." Micah drew a long line in the dirt.

"Who wants to go first?" he asked, holding up a shiny marble.

"Me!" Abigail and Nathaniel and Samuel called simultaneously.

"No, me!" Benjamin shouted, staring up into his cousin's face. "I'm not dead anymore."

In the lands and times of the Bible, people had little time for recreation. Children were pressed into work at an early age, and adults labored nearly from sunup to sundown. That's not to say that life was all drudgery, with nothing to enliven or refresh people. Besides the rest on the Sabbath, the Israelites enjoyed religious festivals like Passover, Purim, or Pentecost. The birth of a child might spark a family celebration and so would a military victory or a bountiful harvest. Weddings were often lavish affairs, filled with dancing, singing, and merriment. When it came to play, children in ancient times had a variety of toys like dolls, miniature animals, balls, and marbles. They played games like Blind Man's Bluff, Knucklebones, or Mancala. Music also provided people with entertainment, and it was used in worship services as well.

Playtime

Historians say that Hebrew parents would have restricted their children's play with dolls or other like objects because of the command to "not make unto thee any graven image" (Exodus 20:4). But aside from that, children in biblical times probably played just as children have played throughout the centuries. They built things out of mud, water, sand, and sticks and played games with marbles and balls. Children in the streets of Ur played hide and seek or hopscotch (a drawing of hopscotch squares was found among the ruins there) just as long-faced children in Jerusalem played "funeral" in the crowded markets. Countless Jewish lads probably killed Goliath with their slings or defeated the Midianites with their imaginary swords. Little girls played "bride," dressed in their mother's oversized tunics, while out among the olive trees their bandit brothers attacked imaginary caravans with sticks and slings. Because houses were generally dark inside, children played mostly outdoors—on their flat roofs, in cisterns, on the threshing floor, in the streets, and in marketplaces. According to ancient Near Eastern custom, young children played together, but the boys generally separated from the girls at around six or seven years old.

Search the Scriptures

Jesus Christ compared the people of his day to children in the marketplace, playing music but not dancing, mourning but not lamenting (Matthew 11:16-19; Luke 7:31-35). These are the children's games "wedding" and "funeral." A child would play a flute while others imitate a wedding procession. Or, they would go around with long faces, pretending to take part in a funeral.

In the Gospels, Jesus Christ is mocked and beaten by religious leaders. The behavior described in Matthew 26:67, 68; Mark 14:65; and Luke 22:63-65 closely resembles the children's game of blind man's bluff, a game played in New Testament times. A blindfolded person is spun around, then made to find the other players. The mockers may have had this game in mind when they so maligned the Lord Jesus Christ. Later, the Roman soldiers also tortured and mocked Jesus Christ (Matthew 27:29-31). The soldiers might have been imitating another children's game called "King" or "Basileus." The game is won when a child is named king, then given a crown, robe, and scepter.

In New Testament times, foot races were popular. Competitors ran naked or with very little clothing. Runners kept their eyes fixed on the end of the course, where a judge sat holding the victory prize. The apostle Paul is likely referring to this type of foot race in Hebrews 12:1, 2. (See also 1 Corinthians 9:24-27.)

Toys, Games, Music, and Dance

Toys

Aside from imaginative play, children in ancient times played with numerous toys and games like dolls, marbles, and balls, Dolls from ancient times were carved from wood or clay, or were made from linen stuffed with papyrus leaves with strands of beads for hair. Marbles and balls are perhaps the oldest toys known—some marbles discovered in a child's grave date back to 4000 B.C. Balls might be made out of linen or leather stuffed with light material like chaff. Pull toys were also popular in ancient times, and so were hobbyhorses. Metal loops of different sizes and baby rattles filled with pebbles were unearthed near Jerusalem. And we know that Roman children played with toy soldiers, because a number of tiny tin men from the third century B.C. were discovered there.

Psalm 137:2 talks of harps hanging in the willows. Because of their sorrow (they were under Babylonian captivity), musicians could not play. Their hands couldn't remember how to strum their instruments, and their mouths were so dry they couldn't sing. This paints a vivid picture of the captive's sorrow.

The word selah appears more than seventy times in the Psalms, but what does it mean? Some scholars say that the word, which means "to pause" or "to lift up," was a musical flag, indicating when the instruments or the singing should start or begin. But others say that selah was more to mark words rather than music, and that the reader should pause and reflect on what was written.

Women of marriageable age often danced at festivals. According to Near Eastern custom, on those days, it was legal for a man to catch a wife while the woman was dancing. (See Judges 21:18-25.)

Coronets or trumpets made out of animal horns were used at sacrifice, wars, or in the temple. The sound was made by air being forcefully blown through a tiny hole. Victorious soldiers entered their city by blowing their horns skyward. If defeated, they blew the horns into the ground. Speaking of the Lord Jesus Christ, Zechariah said, "[God] hath raised up a horn of salvation for us in the house of his servant David...being delivered out of the hand of our enemies" (see Luke 1:68-80).

Games and Riddles

According to ancient drawings, girls played a type of ball game where the penalty for dropping the ball was to carry your opponent on your back! Other games with roots in antiquity include blind man's bluff, leapfrog, and hopscotch. Knucklebones, a precursor to jacks, was evidently popular among girls. Adults and children enjoyed board games like Mancala, chess, and the ancient Egyptian game "Hounds and Jackals," which resembled cribbage. In Greece, they played "Pente," which can still be found in stores today. People in Old Testament times might have tried their hand at the so-called "Royal Game of Ur," one of the oldest games known.

Ancient Near Eastern people were fond of games of skill, strength, and intelligence, especially solving riddles. Perhaps the best-known riddle in history is the one Samson told to the Philistines, "Out of the eater came forth meat, and out of the strong came forth sweetness" (Judges 14:14). The prophet Ezekiel once used a riddle to teach Israel God's Word (Ezekiel 17:2). And biblical scholars believe that the Queen of Sheba posed many riddles to Solomon, for "hard questions" in 1 Kings 10:1 is the same Hebrew word for "riddle" in Judges 14.

Adults might watch archery contests, athletic competitions, or races for entertainment. Acrobats and jugglers performed for wealthy households or for royalty, and men liked to play games with dice. Many sizes and shapes of dice have been discovered throughout the Bible lands, from four-sided dice in the shape of a pyramid, to two-sided discs, to the familiar six-sided cube used today. In place of dice, people might have used teetotums, spinners with numbers on them. Adults sometimes used dice to gamble, a practice popular among Romans, but dice were also used in the legitimate form of casting lots.

Casting Lots

While no one knows exactly what was used in casting lots—possibly coins, dice, or stones—it was a popular, arbitrary way to make a decision, similar to the modern coin toss. The Israelites, though, believed that the outcome was God's will. Casting lots could also mean casting ballots, or voting (see Acts 1:23-26). In biblical times, lots were cast to divide land (Joshua 18:6-10; 1 Chronicles 26:13,14; Isaiah 34:17), to decide between two or more people (1 Samuel 14:42; 1 Chronicles 25:8, 9; Joel 3:3), to chose a man or men for a particular position (1 Chronicles 24:31; Acts 1:23-26), or to set a time for an event (Esther 3:7; 9:24). Sacrifices might be chosen by lot (Leviticus 16:8), or they were cast to single out a guilty person (Jonah 1:7). Perhaps the best known example in the Bible is when the soldiers cast lots for Jesus' garments (Mark 15:24; Luke 23:34; John 19:24): "And they crucified him, and parted his garments, casting lots: that it might be fulfilled which was spoken by the prophet, They parted my garments among them, and upon my vesture did they cast lots" (Matthew 27:35).

Near Eastern Music:
Psalms

Aside from games, people in ancient times enjoyed many forms of music, both vocal and instrumental. Singing and playing instruments was part of Israel's worship (2 Chronicles 29:28-30), yet it might also be associated with idolatrous practices. For instance, during Nebuchadnezzar's reign, instruments were played to cue the people to bow down and worship an idol (Daniel 3:1-7). Yet during King David's time, David appointed a large group of select musicians expressly for "service of the house of the Lord": "And when the builders laid the foundation of the temple of the Lord, they set the priests in their apparel with trumpets, and the Levites the sons of Asaph with cymbals, to praise the Lord, after the ordinance of David king of Israel. And they sang together by course in praising and giving thanks unto the Lord; because he is good, for his mercy endureth for ever toward Israel. And all the people shouted with a great shout, when they praised the Lord, because the foundation of the house of the Lord was laid" (Ezra 3:10, 11).

For the Israelites, songs were an effective way to pass on history. Children might know about the Hebrews' deliverance from Egypt because their parents taught them to sing Psalm 136, or they might know about God's covenant with Abraham from Psalm 105. From the Song of Deborah and Barak they might remember how God avenged Israel in the days of the Judges (Judges 5:1-31).

The book of Psalms, the largest book in the Bible, is a collection of divinely inspired poetic songs of praise. The Hebrew word for "psalm" also means "praise." Psalms vary in purpose and content. Some were written for specific times, like Psalm 92, which was written for the Sabbath, and Psalms 115-118, which were sung during Passover. Some are considered hymns, or songs of praise, while others give thanks for specific acts of God. Others are mournful songs, where an individual or nation asks God for deliverance (for example, Psalm 6 and 79). (For a detailed study on the book of Psalms, see E.W. Bullinger's *The Chief Musician: Or, Studies in the Psalms and Their Titles*.)

Aside from being used in worship, music might be played at any joyous occasion like a coronation (2 Chronicles 23:13), a birth, a religious festival, or a wedding. Dirges or similar somber music would be played at funerals. A victorious army was sure to be greeted by musicians, singers, and possibly dancers when they returned home, like David was after his defeat of the Philistines (1 Samuel 18:6,7).

Sometimes a band of musicians (usually drummers and trumpeters) would be set in front of an army before they went into battle. In the Old Testament, King Jehoshophat appointed singers to lead his army into war (2 Chronicles 20:21).

Professional musicians might also be hired to entertain the wealthy, or to incite laborers to finish a task. A monument in Phrygia, for example, shows a lute and trumpet player with their trick monkey performing for a work crew.

"And when he had consulted with the people, he appointed singers unto the Lord, and that should praise the beauty of holiness, as they went out before the army, and to say, Praise the Lord; for his mercy endureth for ever" (2 Chronicles 20:21).

String Instruments

The first mention of musical instruments in the Bible is in Genesis 4:21, "Jubal. . . the father of all such as handle the harp and organ." While there are enough instruments mentioned in the Bible to fill an orchestra, no one knows for certain exactly what each individual piece looked like. However, the Bible does provide us with some clues as to how instruments sounded or were played. For instance, the harp is mentioned throughout the Bible; it's the instrument David played so well (1 Samuel 16:16, 23). We know this string instrument could sound joyful (Psalm 98:5, 6; Isaiah 24:8), solemn (Psalm 92:3), mournful (Isaiah 16:11), sweet (Isaiah 23:16), and soothing enough to relieve Saul of his spiritual affliction (1 Samuel 16:16, 23). Not only did David play the harp, so did certain prophets (1 Samuel 10:5) and Levites (2 Chronicles 29:25; Nehemiah 12:27). The harp was played in worship and in praise in the temple (Psalm 33:2; 43:4; 1 Chronicles 25:6). It accompanied song and dance (Psalm 149:3) as well as certain prophetic messages (1 Chronicles 25:1-3, 1 Samuel 10:5).

Historians say another string instrument, possibly the biblical dulcimer, looked like a small piano. According to ancient drawings, this odd-shaped box had three strands (made of lamb's gut or horsehair) stretched across an opening at the top. Notes were produced by strumming or striking the cords with mallets. Another type of string instrument had a twenty-four-inch-long neck made of ebony with inlaid ivory and a body made from a hollowed out co-

conut covered with fish skin! Banjo-like instruments with long, skinny necks and round bodies have also been discovered from ancient times, and so have instruments that were played with a bow, similar to the modern cello or viola.

Wind Instruments

Did you know that bagpipes have origins in the ancient Near East? Those used in lands and times of the Bible were made from a whole sheepskin. The player blew through one hole, and the sound was produced through two reeds stuck in another hole. Some say that the biblical "organ" might be this sort of bagpipe (Genesis 4:21; Job 21:12; 30:31; Psalm 150:4). Flutes (called "pipes" in the King James Version) were made from reeds, then later from wood, brass, bone, or ivory. Drawings on an Egyptian monument show a man playing an eighteen-inch-long reed with six holes, holding the instrument to the left side of his body—opposite to how flutes are played today. These wind instruments were played both in secular and sacred settings (see also 1 Samuel 10:5; 1 Kings 1:40; Isaiah 5:12; 30:29; Jeremiah 48:36).

Coronets and trumpets were among the loudest wind instruments of ancient times. Coronets, made from animal horns, were curved while trumpets were ordinarily long and straight. Rams horns, or shofars, were used in Jewish worship, as they are today. These instruments played a significant role in felling the walls of Jericho (Joshua 6) and in defeating the Midianite army (Judges 7). Trumpets were used to announce important news, to sound an alarm, to signal the start of war, or to announce feasts (Psalm 81:3). In the Old Testament, Moses made two silver trumpets to call together the assembly of Israel, and to announce a move in camps (Numbers 10:2). According to Scripture, a trumpet will announce the Second Coming of Christ!

"In a moment, in the twinkling of an eye, at the last trump: for the trumpet shall sound, and the dead shall be raised incorruptible, and we shall be changed." 1 Corinthians 15:52

"For the Lord himself shall descend from heaven with a shout, with the voice of the archangel, and with the trump of God: and the dead in Christ shall rise first." (1 Thessalonians 4:16)

Percussion Instruments

Drums, tambourines, and metal bars of variant lengths and pitches, along with metal triangles and cymbals, are some of the percussion instruments that were used in ancient times. Kettledrums, made from brass or copper kettles with sheep's gut stretched over the top, were played either by hand or by using wooden mallets or sticks. Historians say that drums of all shapes and sizes have been used throughout history, usually in a military context, although drums were also played at festivals. Metal castanets and cymbals, as well as tambourines made from wood, bone, and metal, have been discovered throughout the Bible lands. Called "timbrels" in the Bible, ancient tambourines resembled those used today. The Israelites used tambourines in songs of praise and worship and played them at certain celebrations, too (Exodus 15:20; Psalms 81:2; 149:3; 150:4).

Music and Dancing

In ancient Near Eastern cultures, dancing often accompanied music, and the two are sometimes mentioned together in Scripture (see Exodus 15:20, 21; 1 Samuel 18:6, 7; 2 Samuel 6:14, 15; Psalm 149:3; 150:4). Dance might be associated with legitimate religious celebration or with idolatrous practices. For instance, David danced for joy "before the Lord with all his might" (2 Samuel 6:14), yet the rebellious Hebrews danced before the golden idol (Exodus 32:19). People danced at festivals or at other times of rejoicing like during grape harvest.

In many Near Eastern cultures, women danced only with other women and not with men (see Jeremiah 31:13). For instance, Miriam and other Hebrew women danced together in praise after God parted the Red Sea (Exodus 15:20). The daughters of Shiloh were dancing together when the Benjamites took them (Judges 21:21-23). In some cultures, only marriageable girls would dance in public, for a married woman might be considered immodest if she were to dance in front of other men. Ancient Near Eastern people customarily danced to celebrate military victories, too. For Israel, dancing and singing could be an expression of their praise and worship to God.

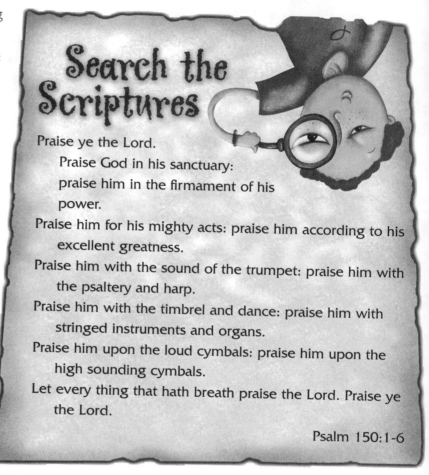

Search the Scriptures

Praise ye the Lord.
   Praise God in his sanctuary: praise him in the firmament of his power.
Praise him for his mighty acts: praise him according to his excellent greatness.
Praise him with the sound of the trumpet: praise him with the psaltery and harp.
Praise him with the timbrel and dance: praise him with stringed instruments and organs.
Praise him upon the loud cymbals: praise him upon the high sounding cymbals.
Let every thing that hath breath praise the Lord. Praise ye the Lord.

Psalm 150:1-6

Make Your Own Praise Band

Throughout the Bible there are references to using various musical instruments when praising God. Ask your students who among them takes music lessons or plays a musical instrument. Pick a session that your class can form a praise band. Have students who can bring their instruments to do so (if your area does not have a piano, arrange to have one moved into your room beforehand). Prior to that date, have the class spend some time making simple musical instruments so that those who do not play an instrument will have one for the praise band. Here are some suggestions for making simple musical instruments that are similar to those used in Bible times.

REED FLUTES

Many people will recognize the soft whine of a reed flute as being part of the Middle East.

Materials Needed:

- a plastic drinking straw
- a sheet of paper
- scissors

Instructions:

1. Flatten and trim about ¼ inch to ⅜ inch off each side of one end of the drinking straw so that it looks something like a bird's beak (not quite a sharp point, but close).
2. Roll the paper into a cone that has an opening at one end that is an inch or two in diameter and an opening at the other end that will fit around the straw snugly. Tape the edges of the paper to form the cone.
3. Snip off about an inch or so of the trimmed straw and tape it in the smaller opening of the cone with the v-shaped end as a mouthpiece. If the straw is too rigid, you may have to

flatten it a bit around the trimmed area so that it buzzes when you blow through it.

HARP OR LYRE

Materials Needed

- an empty tissue box
- 6 to 8 rubber bands
- scissors

Instructions

1. Decorate the box with markers, stickers, glitter, etc., however you want.
2. Notch the top edges of the box to keep the rubber bands from rolling off as they are strummed.
3. Stretch the rubber bands around the box and across the opening. If you use different size rubber bands, you will get different sounds as you strum them.

FINGER CYMBALS

Materials Needed

- two large flat washers with ¼-inch holes
- small rubber bands

Instructions

1. Place a rubber band over your finger.
2. String the bottom end through the washer and loop the end over the end of your finger. You can stretch the rubber band to make it hold the washer flat against your finger.
3. Repeat the procedure for your thumb. Simply click the washers together to the beat of the music.

Games With Ancient Origins

Blind Man's Bluff

Blindfold one person. Move the person around the room until he is disoriented. The blindfolded person has to find and identify each person without looking.

Piggyback Ball Game

Children toss a ball around in a circle. If someone drops the ball, they must then carry the thrower on their back. The person being carried then gets to throw the ball. The game continues until everyone has dropped the ball—or they collapse!

Inside the Circle
(A.K.A. "DODGE BALL")

Using a long rope (or garden hose), make a large circle. (Draw one in the sand if you're at a beach.) Children stand inside. The "attacker" stands outside, trying to hit every person with the ball. Any person who is hit is "out." Those in the circle cannot move outside the perimeter. The last person left inside the circle wins and is the next "attacker."

You can modify the game so that once an insider is hit, he becomes an attacker, too. Those remaining inside can now be hit by any person outside the circle. This is a faster-paced version.

Ancient Marble Games

At the bottom of a small slope, dig a hole about 2 inches in diameter. Collect one marble from every player, then toss all the marbles up the hill. Some will fall into the hole (those now belong to the thrower), the rest scatter around the hole. Next, the thrower stands behind a line drawn in the sand (about 4 feet away) and tries to knock into the hole one of the marbles his friends have selected for him. He can hit only that marble, and nothing else. If he succeeds, he wins all the marbles. If he hits any other marble, he loses all the marbles that he got in the hole. After his turn is over, it's the next persons turn. Turns continue until all the marbles are claimed.

Dig a hole about 3 inches in diameter and draw a line about 4 feet away. Players sit on the ground behind the line. Using one finger to flick the marble, each player will in turn try to shoot his marble into the hole. Some will roll into the hole while others will be scattered around the hole.

Those whose marbles made it into the hole get a chance to capture the rest of the marbles. Each person takes his marble out of the hole and places it outside the edge. With his thumb in the hole, he flicks the marble with his middle finger, trying to hit any other marble nearby. He keeps those he hits, and he continues on until he misses. If he misses, his marble stays on the ground, prey to the next shooter.

Projects Using Terra-cotta Clay

Just as in modern days, children of Bible times liked to play with clay and mud. There are many archaeological finds of clay toys, including balls, dice, dolls, and carts. Have your class relive the fun by allowing them to make toys out of clay.

Clay Games

In order to play different games, Middle Eastern children would make game boards, dice, and other game pieces out of clay. Have your class make clay checker boards and checkers or tic-tac-toe boards and clay X and O pieces. Or have your class form a pair of dice: six-sided cubes, two-sided discs, or four-sided pyramid shapes. Indent holes to indicate numbers on each side. Let dry, then paint the indentations. These can be used with regular board games or with games you make up as a class.

Clay Ox Cart

Just as today, children in Bible times played at working. While kids today play with cars and trucks, children in ancient times would make small carts to play with. These were more representations of real carts, and most likely did not have movable wheels. Have your class make two wheels about the size of a half dollar. Using twigs, leaves, or anything else from the outdoors, make a cart bed and attach it to the wheels before the clay hardens.

Clay Figurines

Clay figures were among the first dolls that ancient children played with. Representing babies, soldiers, and animals, clay figurines were popular playthings. Have your class fashion miniature animals: pigs, horses, ducks, sheep, etc. Try making miniature furnishings, such as lamps, plates, bowls, jars, etc., for the mud-brick house shown on page 24.

Classroom Exercises

1. Study the phrase "hard sayings" or "riddles" in the Bible.
2. Write out a verse on a large piece of construction paper, then cut the paper into pieces. Have students reassemble the puzzle.
3. Separate students into two teams. Have one team devise a riddle and the other team solve it. Or, find a book of riddles and do the same.
4. Study all the uses of the word selah.
5. Set one of the Psalms to music.
6. Separate boys and girls into two groups. Have each team devise a dance, based on a biblical story. Have each team perform their dance, then see if the other team can guess what story it is.

Make a Bow and Arrow

Materials Needed:

- Plastic string (or guitar string)
- Carving knife
- green sticks or branches

Directions:

1. To make a bow, find a large, flexible branch that bends easily into an arch.
2. Tie a string tightly from one end of the branch to the other, forcing it into an arch.
3. To make arrows, find several straight twigs, about 24 inches long and ¼ to ⅜ inch in diameter.
4. Sharpen to a point one end of each arrow with knife and cut a notch at the other end. (Keep in mind that bows and arrows are not toys; they are ancient weapons. Be certain that your students make and use bows and arrows safely.)

Making a Ball

This project will resemble more of a beanbag or pillow, but if you stuff it with enough materials, it will get pretty round. This beats using clay, wood, stone, or even glass balls, all of which have been found in various archaeological sites. Some archaeologists have found leather examples of balls made similar to this project; a number of these balls were stitched like modern soccer balls, with many different hexagonal and pentagonal pieces to create a ball that is almost perfectly round.

Materials Needed:

- ½ yard heavy fabric
- needle and thread
- batting or some other filler
- scissors

Directions:

1. Using the pattern provided, sketch out the form on the fabric and cut it out, being sure to leave it as one piece.
2. Stitch together the sides of each of the points, leaving about an inch or so open on one side to stuff the ball. As you stitch, the ball will begin to take shape.
3. Turn the ball inside out.
4. Fill with the batting or another filler (crumpled paper, uncooked macaroni, dried beans, etc.) and stitch the opening shut.

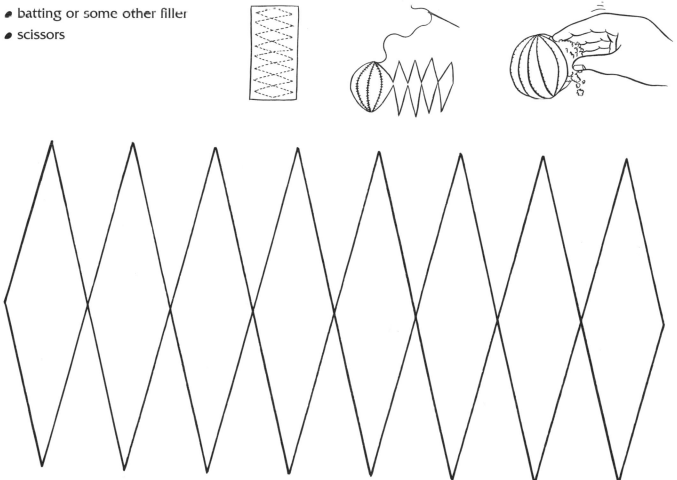

Teetotum

These spinners were used in place of dice and came in many shapes and sizes.

Materials Needed:

- pencil (sharpened)
- cardboard or poster board
- markers
- a ruler
- scissors
- tape

Directions:

1. Using the pattern, make a small box with the poster board or cardboard, marking each side with a number.
2. Run the pencil through the middle of the cube.
3. Spin the pencil. The number facing up is the number chosen.

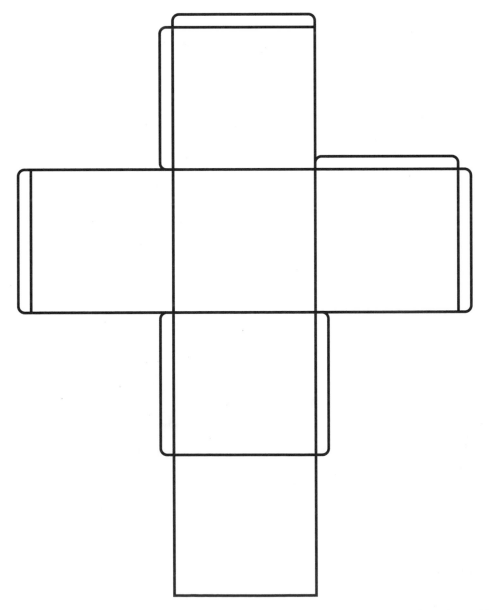

Bibliography

Bouquet, A.C. *Everyday Life in New Testament Times*. New York: Charles Scribners Sons, 1954.

Bullinger, E.W. *The Companion Bible*. Grand Rapids, MI: Kregel Publications, 1990.

————*The Chief Musician: Or, Studies in the Psalms and Their Titles*. Lafayette, IN: Truth for Today Bible Fellowship, 1992.

————*Figures of Speech Used in the Bible*. Grand Rapids, MI: Baker Book House, 1968.

————*The Witness of the Stars*. Grand Rapids, MI: Kregel, 1980.

Burrows, Millar. *The Dead Sea Scrolls*. New York, Viking Press. 1955

Civilizations of the Middle East. Raintree Publishers, Austin, Tx. 1992

Day, Malcolm. *The Ancient World of the Bible*. New York, Viking Press. 1994

Edersheim, Alfred. *The Life and Times of Jesus the Messiah*. Peabody, Ma., Hendrickson Publishing, 1993.

Edmonds, Brian. *Bible Healing Food*. Boca Raton, FL: Globe Communications Corps, 1996.

Everyday Life in Bible Times, James Pritchard, ed. National Geographic Soc.,1967.

Farb, Peter. *The Land, Wildlife, and Peoples of the Bible*. Harper and Row, NY. 1967.

Freeman, James M. *Manners and Customs of the Bible*. Plainfield, NJ. Logos International, 1972.

Gower, Ralph. *The New Manners and Customs of Bible Times*. Chicago: Moody Press, 1987.

Harper's Bible Dictionary, Cambridge, Ma. Harper and Row, 1985

Heaton, E.W. *Everyday Life in Old Testament Times*. New York: Charles Scribner & Sons, 1956.

Illustrated Bible Dictionary, Vols. 1-3. Tyndale House, Leicester, England. 1994.

Jesus and His Times. Reader's Digest, Kaori Ward, ed. 1987.

Mackie, George M. *Bible Manners and Customs*. New York: Fleming H. Revell Co., (no date)

Mason, Anthony. *If You Were There in Biblical Times*. New York: Simon & Schuster, 1996.

Matthews, Victor H. *Manners and Customs In the Bible*. Peabody, MA: Hendrickson Publishers Inc., 1997.

Odijik, Pamela. *The Israelites*. Silver Burdett Press, Englewood Cliffs, NJ. 1989.

Pillai, Bishop K.C. *Light Through an Eastern Window*. New York, Robert Speller and Sons Publishers, 1963.

———— *Orientalisms of the Bible*: Volumes 1,2. Fairborn, OH. Mor-Mac Publishing Co., Inc. 1966, 1974

Rearhard, Bo. *The Eastern Customs and Manners of the Bible and Their Spiritual Application in Understanding the Scriptures*. New Knoxville, OH: American Christian Press, 1980.

Rice, Edwin Wilbur. *Orientalisms in the Bible*. Philadelphia: American Sunday School Union, 1910.

Smith, Joan Ripley. *Growing Up Where Jesus Lived*. Pensacola, FL: A Beka Book, 1988.

The Book of the Bible. Rev. James Roe, ed., Golden Press. 1972.

Thomson, William M. *The Land and the Book: Volumes 1-3*. New York: Harper and Brothers, 1882.

Tubb, Jonathan N. *Bible Lands*. New York: Knopf Publishers,1991.

Van-Lennep, Henry J. *Bible Lands: Their Modern Customs and Manners Illustrative of Scripture*. New York, Harper and Brothers. 1875

White, Gwen. *Antique Toys and Their Background*. New York: Arco Publishing Co., 1971.

Wierwille, Victor Paul. *Jesus Christ Our Passover*. New Knoxville, OH: American Christian Press, 1980.

———— *Jesus Christ Our Promised Seed*. New Knoxville, OH: American Christian Press, 1982.

Wight, Fred H. *Manners and Customs of Bible Lands*. Chicago. Moody Press, 1953.

Index